EUGENE O'NEILL

The Emperor Jones

THE STRAW *and* DIFF'RENT

Three Plays

JONATHAN CAPE

THIRTY BEDFORD SQUARE LONDON

FIRST PUBLISHED 1922
THIS PAPERBACK EDITION FIRST PUBLISHED 1969
REPRINTED 1975, 1978

JONATHAN CAPE LTD, 30 BEDFORD SQUARE, LONDON WC1

ISBN 0 224 61641 2

Printed in Great Britain by
Lowe & Brydone Printers Limited, Thetford, Norfolk

JONATHAN CAPE
PAPERBACK
JCP 71

THE EMPEROR JONES

Introduction

I DO not think I am exaggerating when I say that Eugene O'Neill, of whose collected plays this is the first volume, is the most significant American dramatist of to-day. Practically a post-War discovery—an early volume of his plays appeared in Boston in 1914, but New York knew him only in 1919—he has quickly gained recognition in his own country. At first the Provincetown Players, a group of semi-professional actors interested in new plays, put on some of his one-act pieces in their wharf theatre; then they introduced him to New York in an equally primitive setting in Greenwich Village; and a larger New York public was soon privileged to see his *Beyond the Horizon* at an up-town theatre. It was an immediate success and was quickly followed by his *The Emperor Jones*, *Diff'rent*, and *Gold*. During the last year *Diff'rent* and his little one-act play of the sea, *In the Zone*, have been produced in London by the Everyman company, and Mr. C. B. Cochran promises a production of *The Emperor Jones*, his most mature work. If O'Neill can continue to write plays as excellent as this last, it seems certain that within a very short time he will be recognised as one of the greatest living writers of English drama.

Of Eugene O'Neill the man I know little. He avoids personal publicity and is rarely to be found in towns. Nevertheless, one continually hears things about him that throw light upon his personality. One knows at least that he is the son of a well-known

American actor, the late James O'Neill; he is just over thirty years of age, and has led a roving life as a clerk, a gold prospector in Honduras, an actor, a reporter, and an able seaman; the last might be guessed from the predominance of sea motives in his earlier plays. A friend of mine has told me of a characteristic meeting with him some years ago in a sailors' dive in Buenos Ayres, where O'Neill was stranded after a voyage. To-day he lives in a desolate old coastguard station near Provincetown, Massachusetts.

The three plays in this volume, *The Straw*, *The Emperor Jones*, and *Diff'rent*, are a happy first selection. They represent three varied styles in which he has worked, and although, of course, they do not give by any means a complete view of his many-sided talent, they are a useful introduction to him for English readers. *The Straw* shows him as a writer of more or less conventional drama. It is the story of a consumptive girl, her family and her lovers; if all the scenes are not of equal merit, the best of them make a strong dramatic appeal. The reader, I trust, in this as in the other pieces, will not object to occasional Americanisms in an American play. He must decide for himself whether the play concludes with what is known as a happy ending; it is, I fancy, the only one of all O'Neill's grim dramas in which this question is even possible.

Diff'rent is a psychological play—" a study of a sex-starved woman " is an accurate American description of it. Anyone who knows how greatly America to-day is interested in psychological research will realise how O'Neill came to write a play of this nature; unlike most pieces dealing with such themes, it goes remarkably well in a theatre, as both London and New York playgoers have discovered.

But it is to *The Emperor Jones* that I should most wish to draw the reader's attention. I do not know to what extent I shall find agreement, but in my opinion this is in several respects one of the most interesting plays that have been written in recent years. As a theatrical spectacle it is certainly unique in my experience of theatre-going. One may say of most plays that their appeal is as readily felt in print as in the theatre; for many of them moreover the arm-chair is the only actor-proof setting. But there are some plays which in the theatre have additional qualities to those they hold in print, and it is among these that *The Emperor Jones* takes high rank. It enthralls the listener; I noticed in New York how even during the *entr'actes* the audience continued to feel its dramatic quality; a realisation of tragedy kept one in one's seat awaiting the further unfolding of the story. The theatre ceased for a moment to be a social function and became again a temple of of mystery and fate.

Technically, too, *The Emperor Jones* is of great interest. For years dramatists have been attempting to find a new kind of play, something that would pass beyond the limits of the usual contemporary drama. Russians especially have tried to establish such new forms; "monodrama," "kinemodrama" and others are among the experiments they have made. But in *The Emperor Jones* O'Neill may be said to have solved this problem. The play is practically a monologue spoken by the principal character; the other persons appear only in the first and last scenes, fulfilling the function of chorus to his tragedy. The sound of the tomtom beaten by his pursuers is the antagonist in this drama of fear. The reader will notice the skill with which the character of the negro Pullman-car porter turned

Emperor is drawn; the quaint thoughts and turns of speech; the cynical bombast and genuine dignity; the conflict of his intelligence, developed in everyday life and religious teaching, with the ingrained superstitions of his race. That Emperor Jones is a character unique in literature goes without saying; and the play to which he gives his name is as rare as he is.

The principal dramatic works of Eugene O'Neill are as follows :—

> *Thirst*
> *The Web*
> *Warnings*
> *Fog*
> *Recklessness*
> *The Moon of the Caribbees*   One Act Plays
> *Bound East for Cardiff*
> *The Long Voyage Home*
> *In the Zone*
> *Ile*
> *Where the Cross is Made*
> *The Rope*
> *Gold*
> *Chris. Christopherson*
> *Beyond the Horizon*
> *The Old Davil*
> *The Straw*
> *Diff'rent*
> *Emperor Jones*
> *Anna Christie*
> *The Hairy Ape* (produced March 1922)

C. E. BECHHOFER

London *April*, 1922

viii

Contents

The Straw

Characters

BILL CARMODY
MARY
NORA
TOM } *his children*
BILLY
DOCTOR GAYNOR,
FRED NICHOLLS,
EILEEN CARMODY, *Bill's eldest child*
STEPHEN MURRAY,
MISS HOWARD, *a nurse in training*
MISS GILPIN, *superintendent of the Infirmary*
DOCTOR STANTON, *of the Hill Farm Sanatorium*
DOCTOR SIMMS, *his assistant*
MR. SLOAN
PETERS, *a patient*
MRS. TURNER, *matron of the Sanatorium*
MISS BAILEY
MRS. ABNER } *Patients*
FLYNN
OTHER PATIENTS OF THE SANATORIUM
MRS. BRENNAN

(The characters are named in the order in which they
appear)

Act One

Scene One: The Kitchen of the Carmody Home—
Evening.
Scene Two: The Reception Room of the Infirmary,
Hill Farm Sanatorium—An Evening a Week
Later.

Act Two

Scene One: Assembly Room of the Main Building at
the Sanatorium—A Morning Four Months
Later.
Scene Two: A Crossroads Near the Sanatorium—
Midnight of the Same Day.

Act Three

An Isolation Room and Porch at the Sanatorium—
An Afternoon Four Months Later.

Time—1910

The Straw
Act One

Act One : Scene One

*The kitchen of the Carmody home on the outskirts of a
manufacturing town in Connecticut. On the left,
forward, the sink. Farther back, two windows
looking out on the yard. In the left corner, rear,
the icebox. Immediately to the right of it, in the
rear wall, a window opening on the side porch. To
the right of this, a china cupboard, and a door leading
into the hall where the main front entrance to the
house and the stairs to the floor above are situated.
On the right, to the rear, a door opening on to the
dining room. Further forward, the kitchen range
with scuttle, wood box, etc. In the centre of the
room, a table with a red and white cloth. Four
cane-bottomed chairs are pushed under the table.
In front of the stove, two battered wicker rocking chairs. The floor is partly covered by linoleum
strips. The walls are papered a light cheerful colour. Several old framed picture-supplement
prints hang from nails. Everything has a clean,
neatly-kept appearance. The supper dishes are
piled in the sink ready for washing. A saucepan of
water simmers on the stove.*

It is about eight o'clock in the evening of a

bitter cold day in late February of the year 1912.

As the curtain rises, Bill Carmody is discovered sitting in a rocker by the stove, reading a newspaper and smoking a blackened clay pipe. He is a man of fifty, heavy-set and round-shouldered, with long muscular arms and swollen-veined, hairy hands. His face is bony and ponderous ; his nose short and squat ; his mouth large, thick-lipped and harsh ; his complexion mottled—red, purple-streaked, and freckled ; his hair, short and stubby with a bald spot on the crown. The expression of his small, blue eyes is one of selfish cunning. His voice is loud and hoarse. He wears a flannel shirt, open at the neck, criss-crossed by red braces ; black, baggy trousers grey with dust ; muddy brogues.

His youngest daughter, Mary, is sitting on a chair by the table, front, turning over the pages of a picture book. She is a delicate, dark-haired, blue-eyed, quiet little girl about eight years old.

CARMODY (*after watching the child's preoccupation for a moment, in a tone of half exasperated amusement*). Well, but you're the quiet one, surely ! (*Mary looks up at him with a shy smile, her eyes still full of dreams.*) Glory be to God, I'd not know a soul was alive in the room, barrin' myself. What is it you're at, Mary, that there's not a word out of you ?

MARY. I'm looking at the pictures.

CARMODY. It's the dead spit and image of your sister Eileen you are, with your nose always in a book ; and you're like your mother, too, God rest her soul. (*He crosses himself with pious unction and Mary*

8

also does so.) It's Nora and Tom has the high spirits in them like their father; and Billy, too,—if he is a lazy, shiftless divil—has the fightin' Carmody blood like me. You're a Cullen like your mother's people. They always was dreamin' their lives out. (*He lights his pipe and shakes his head with ponderous gravity*.) There's no good in too many books, I'll tell you. It's out rompin' and playin' with your brother and sister you ought to be at your age, not carin' a fig for books. (*With a glance at the clock*.) Is that auld fool of a doctor stayin' the night? If he had his wits about him he'd know in a jiffy 'tis only a cold has taken Eileen, and give her the medicine. Run out in the hall, Mary, and see if you hear him. He may have sneaked away by the front door.

MARY (*goes out into the hall, rear, and comes back*). He's upstairs. I heard him talking to Eileen.

CARMODY. Close the door, ye little divil! There's a freezin' draught comin' in. (*She does so and comes back to her chair. Carmody continues with a sneer*.) It's mad I am to be thinkin' he'd go without gettin' his money—the like of a doctor! (*Angrily*.) Rogues and thieves they are, the lot of them, robbin' the poor like us! I've no use for their drugs at all. They only keep you sick to pay more visits. I'd not have sent for this bucko if Eileen didn't scare me by faintin'.

MARY (*anxiously*). Is Eileen very sick, Papa?

CARMODY (*spitting—roughly*). If she is, it's her own fault entirely—weakenin' her health by readin' here in the house. This'll be a lesson for her, and for you,

9

too. (*Irritably.*) Put down that book on the table and leave it be. I'll have no more readin' in this house, or I'll take the strap to you!

MARY (*laying the book on the table*). It's only pictures.

CARMODY. No back talk! Pictures or not, it's all the same mopin' and lazin' in it. (*After a pause—morosely.*) It's the bad luck I've been havin' altogether this last year since your mother died. Who's to do the work and look after Nora and Tom and yourself, if Eileen is bad took and has to stay in her bed? I'll have to get Mrs. Brennan come look after the house. That means money, too, and where's it to come from? All that I've saved from slavin' and sweatin' in the sun with a gang of lazy Dagoes'll be up the spout in no time. (*Bitterly.*) What a fool a man is to be raisin' a raft of children and him not a millionaire! (*With lugubrious self-pity.*) Mary, dear, it's a black curse God put on me when he took your mother just when I needed her most. (*Mary commences to sob. Carmody starts and looks at her angrily.*) What are you sniffin' at?

MARY (*tearfully*). I was thinking—of Mamma.

CARMODY (*scornfully*). It's late you are with your tears, and her cold in her grave for a year. Stop it, I'm tellin' you! (*Mary gulps back her sobs.*)

> (*There is a noise of childish laughter and screams from the street in front. The outside door is opened and slammed, footsteps pound along the hall. The door in the rear is pushed open, and Nora and Tom*

rush in breathlessly. Nora is a bright, vivacious, red-haired girl of eleven—pretty after an elfish, mischievous fashion—light-hearted and robust.)

(Tom resembles Nora in disposition and appearance. A healthy, good-humoured youngster with a shock of sandy hair. He is a year younger than Nora. They are followed into the room, a moment later, by their brother Billy, who is evidently loftily disgusted with their antics. Billy is a fourteen-year-old replica of his father, whom he imitates even to the hoarse, domineering tone of voice.)

CARMODY (*grumpily*). Ah, here you are, the lot of you. Shut that door after you! What's the use in me spendin' money for coal if all you do is to let the cold night in the room itself?

NORA (*hopping over to him—teasingly*). Me and Tom had a race, Papa. I beat him. (*She sticks her tongue out at her younger brother.*) Slow poke!

TOM. You didn't beat me, neither!

NORA. I did, too!

TOM. You did not! You didn't play fair. You tripped me comin' up the steps. Brick-top! Cheater!

NORA (*flaring up*). You're a liar! You stumbled over your own big feet, clumsy bones! And I beat you fair. Didn't I, Papa?

CARMODY (*with a grin*). You did, darlin', and fair, too. (*Tom slinks back to the chair in the rear*

11

f table, sulking. Carmody pats Nora's red hair with delighted pride.) Sure it's you can beat the divil himself!

NORA (*sticks out her tongue again at Tom.*) See? Liar! (*She goes and perches on the table near Mary, who is staring sadly in front of her.*)

CARMODY (*to Billy—irritably*). Did you get the plug for me I told you?

BILLY. Sure. (*He takes a plug of tobacco from his pocket and hands it to his father. Nora slides down off her perch and disappears, unnoticed, under the table.*)

CARMODY. It's a great wonder you didn't forget it—and me without a chew. (*He bites off a piece and tucks it into his cheek.*)

TOM (*suddenly clutching at his leg with a yell*). Ouch! Darn you! (*He kicks frantically at something under the table, but Nora scrambles out at the other end, grinning.*)

CARMODY (*angrily*). Shut your big mouth! What is the matter with you at all?

TOM (*indignantly*). She pinched me—hard as she could, too—and look at her laughin'!

NORA (*hopping on the table again*). Cry-baby! I owed you one.

TOM. I'll fix you. I'll tell Eileen, wait 'n' see!

NORA. Tattle-tale! I don't care. Eileen's sick.

TOM. That's why you dast do it. You dasn't if she was up. I'll get even, you bet!

CARMODY (*exasperated*). Shut up your noise! Go

up to bed, the two of you, and no more talk, and you go with them, Mary.

NORA (*giving a quick tug at Mary's hair*). Come on, Mary. Wake up.

MARY. Ow! (*She begins to cry.*)

CARMODY (*raising his voice furiously*). Hush your noise, you soft, weak thing, you! It's nothin' but blubberin' you do be doin' all the time. (*He stands up threateningly.*) I'll have a moment's peace, I will! Off to bed with you before I get the strap! It's crazy mad you all get the moment Eileen's away from you. Go on, now! (*They scurry out of the rear door.*) And be quiet or I'll be up to you!

NORA (*sticks her head back in the door*). Can I say good-night to Eileen, Papa?

CARMODY. No. The doctor's with her yet. (*Then he adds hastily.*) Yes, go in to her, Nora. It'll drive himself out of the house maybe, bad cess to him, and him stayin' half the night. (*Nora waits to hear no more but darts back, shutting the door behind her. Billy takes the chair in front of the table. Carmody sits down again with a groan.*) The rheumatics are in my leg again. (*Shakes his head.*) If Eileen's in bed long those brats'll have the house down.

BILLY. Eileen ain't sick very bad, is she?

CARMODY (*easily*). It's a cold only she has. (*Then mournfully.*) Your poor mother died of the same. (*Billy looks awed.*) Ara, well, it's God's will, I suppose, but where the money'll come from, I dunno. (*With

13

a disparaging glance at his son.) They'll not be raisin' your wages soon, I'll be bound.

BILLY (*surlily*). Naw. The old boss never gives no one a raise, 'less he has to. He's a tight-wad for fair.

CARMODY (*still scanning him with contempt*). Five dollars a week—for a strappin' lad the like of you! It's shamed you should be to own up to it. A divil of a lot of good it was for me to go against Eileen's wish and let you leave off your schoolin' this year like you wanted, thinkin' the money you'd earn at work would help with the house.

BILLY. Aw, goin' to school didn't do me no good. The teachers was all down on me. I couldn't learn nothin' there.

CARMODY (*disgustedly*). Nor any other place, I'm thinkin', you're that thick. (*There is a noise from the stairs in the hall.*) Whisht! It's the doctor comin' down from Eileen. What'll he say, I wonder? (*The door in the rear is opened and Doctor Gaynor enters. He is a stout, bald, middle-aged man, forceful of speech, who in the case of patients of the Carmodys' class dictates rather than advises. Carmody adopts a whining tone.*) Aw, Doctor, and how's Eileen now? Have you got her cured of the weakness?

GAYNOR (*does not answer this but comes forward into the room holding out two slips of paper—dictatorially*). Here are two prescriptions that'll have to be filled immediately.

CARMODY (*frowning*). You take them, Billy, and

14

run round to the drug store. (*Gaynor hands them to Billy.*)

BILLY.   Give me the money, then.

CARMODY (*reaches down into his trousers pocket with a sigh*).   How much will they come to, Doctor?

GAYNOR.   About a dollar, I guess.

CARMODY (*protestingly*).   A dollar! Sure it's expensive medicines you're givin' her for a bit of a cold. (*He meets the doctor's cold glance of contempt and he wilts—grumblingly, as he peels a dollar bill off a small roll and gives it to Billy.*) Bring back the change—if there is any. And none of your tricks, for I'll stop at the drug store myself to-morrow and ask the man how much it was.

BILLY.   Aw, what do you think I am? (*He takes the money and goes out.*)

CARMODY (*grudgingly*).   Take a chair, Doctor, and tell me what's wrong with Eileen.

GAYNOR (*seating himself by the table—gravely*).   Your daughter is very seriously ill.

CARMODY (*irritably*).   Aw, Doctor, didn't I know you'd be sayin' that, anyway!

GAYNOR (*ignoring this remark — coldly*).   Your daughter has tuberculosis of the lungs.

CARMODY (*with puzzled awe*).   Too-ber-c'losis?

GAYNOR.   Consumption, if that makes it plainer to you.

CARMODY (*with dazed terror—after a pause*).

15

Consumption? Eileen? (*With sudden anger.*) What lie is it you're tellin' me?

GAYNOR (*icily*). Look here, Carmody! I'm not here to stand for your insults!

CARMODY (*bewilderingly*). Don't be angry, now, at what I said. Sure I'm out of my wits entirely. Eileen to have the consumption! Ah, Doctor, sure you must be mistaken!

GAYNOR. There's no chance for a mistake, I'm sorry to say. Her right lung is badly affected.

CARMODY (*desperately*). It's a bad cold only, maybe.

GAYNOR (*curtly*). Don't talk nonsense. (*Carmody groans. Gaynor continues authoritatively.*) She will have to go to a sanatorium at once. She ought to have been sent to one months ago. The girl's been keeping up on her nerve when she should have been in bed, and it's given the disease a chance to develop. (*Casts a look of indignant scorn at Carmody, who is sitting staring at the floor with an expression of angry stupor on his face.*) It's a wonder to me you didn't see the condition she was in and force her to take care of herself. Why, the girl's nothing but skin and bone!

CARMODY (*with vague fury*). God blast it!

GAYNOR. No, your kind never realises things till the crash comes—usually when it's too late. She kept on doing her work, I suppose—taking care of her brothers and sisters, washing, cooking, sweeping, looking after your comfort—worn out—when she should have been in bed—and—— (*He gets to his*

16

feet with a harsh laugh.) But what's the use of talking ? The damage is done. We've got to set to work to repair it at once. I'll write to-night to Dr. Stanton of the Hill Farm Sanatorium and find out if he has a vacancy. And if luck is with us we can send her there at once. The sooner the better.

CARMODY (*his face growing red with rage*). Is it sendin' Eileen away to a hospital you'd be ? (*Exploding.*) Then you'll not ! You'll get that notion out of your head damn quick. It's all nonsense you're stuffin' me with, and lies, makin' things out to be the worst in the world. I'll not believe a word of Eileen having the consumption at all. It's doctors' notions to be always lookin' for a sickness that'd kill you. She'll not move a step out of here, and I say so, and I'm her father !

GAYNOR (*who has been staring at him with contempt—coldly angry*). You refuse to let your daughter go to a sanatorium ?

CARMODY. I do.

GAYNOR (*threateningly*). Then I'll have to report her case to the Society for the Prevention of Tuberculosis of this county, and tell them of your refusal to help her.

CARMODY (*wavering a bit*). Report all you like, and be damned to you !

GAYNOR (*ignoring the interruption—impressively*). A majority of the most influential men of this city are behind the Society. Do you know that ? (*Grimly.*) We'll find a way to move you, Carmody, if you try to be stubborn.

CARMODY (*thoroughly frightened, but still protesting*). Ara, Doctor, you don't see the way of it at all. If Eileen goes to the hospital, who's to be takin' care of the others, and mindin' the house when I'm off to work?

GAYNOR. You can easily hire some woman.

CARMODY (*at once furious again*). Hire? D'you think I'm a millionaire itself?

GAYNOR (*contemptuously*). That's where the shoe pinches, eh? (*In a rage.*) I'm not going to waste any more words on you, Carmody, but I'm damn well going to see this thing through! You might as well give in first as last.

CARMODY (*wailing*). But where's the money comin' from?

GAYNOR (*brutally*). That's your concern. Don't lie about your poverty. You've a steady well-paid job, and plenty of money to throw away on drunken sprees, I'll bet. The weekly fee at the Hill Farm is only seven dollars. You can easily afford that—the price of a few rounds of drinks.

CARMODY. Seven dollars! And I'll have to pay a woman to come in—and the four of the children eatin' their heads off! Glory be to God, I'll not have a penny saved for me old age—and then it's the poor-house!

GAYNOR (*curtly*). Don't talk nonsense!

CARMODY. Ah, doctor, it's the truth I'm tellin' you!

GAYNOR. Well, perhaps I can get the Society to

pay half for your daughter—if you're really as hard up as you pretend. They're willing to do that where it seems necessary.

CARMODY (*brightening*). Ah, Doctor, thank you.

GAYNOR (*abruptly*). Then it's all settled?

CARMODY (*grudgingly—trying to make the best of it*). I'll do my best for Eileen, if it's needful—and you'll not be tellin' them people about it at all, Doctor?

GAYNOR. Not unless you force me to.

CARMODY. And they'll pay the half, surely?

GAYNOR. I'll see what I can do—for your daughter's sake, not yours, understand!

CARMODY. God bless you, Doctor! (*Grumblingly.*) It's the whole of it they ought to be payin', I'm thinkin', and them with bags of money. 'Tis them builds the hospitals and why should they be wantin' the poor like me to support them?

GAYNOR (*disgustedly*). Bah! (*Abruptly.*) I'll telephone to Doctor Stanton to-morrow morning. Then I'll know something definite when I come to see your daughter in the afternoon.

CARMODY (*darkly*). You'll be comin' again to-morrow? (*Half to himself.*) Leave it to the likes of you to be drainin' a man dry.

> (*Gaynor has gone out to the hall in rear and does not hear this last remark. There is a loud knock from the outside door. The Doctor comes back into the room carrying his hat and overcoat.*)

GAYNOR. There's someone knocking.

CARMODY. Who'll it be? Ah, it's Fred Nicholls, maybe. (*In a low voice to Gaynor who has started to put on his overcoat.*) Eileen's young man, Doctor, that she's engaged to marry, as you might say.

GAYNOR (*thoughtfully*). H'mm—yes—she spoke of him.

> (*As another knock sounds Carmody hurries to the rear. Gaynor, after a moment's indecision, takes off his overcoat again and sits down. A moment later Carmody re-enters, followed by Fred Nicholls, who has left his overcoat and hat in the hallway. Nicholls is a young fellow of twenty-three, stockily built, fair-haired, handsome in a commonplace, conventional mould. His manner is obviously an attempt at suave gentility; he has an easy, taking smile and a ready laugh, but there is a petty, calculating expression in his small, observing, blue eyes. His well-fitting, ready-made clothes are carefully pressed. His whole get-up suggests an attitude of man-about-small-town complacency.*)

CARMODY (*as they enter*). I had a mind to phone to your house, but I wasn't wishful to disturb you, knowin' you'd be comin' to call to-night.

NICHOLLS (*with disappointed concern*). It's nothing serious, I hope.

CARMODY (*grumblingly*). Ah, who knows ? Here's the doctor. You've not met him ?

NICHOLLS (*politely, looking at Gaynor, who inclines his head stiffly*). I haven't had the pleasure. Of course, I've heard——

CARMODY. It's Doctor Gaynor. This is Fred Nicholls, Doctor. (*The two men shake hands with conventional greetings.*) Sit down, Fred, that's a good lad, and be talkin' to the Doctor a moment while I go upstairs and see how is Eileen. She's all alone up there.

NICHOLLS. Certainly, Mr. Carmody. Go ahead—and tell her how sorry I am to learn she's under the weather.

CARMODY. I will so. (*He goes out.*)

GAYNOR (*after a pause in which he is studying Nicholls*). Do you happen to be any relative to the Albert Nicholls who is superintendent over at the Downs Manufacturing Company ?

NICHOLLS (*smiling*). He's sort of a near relative—my father.

GAYNOR. Ah, yes ?

NICHOLLS (*with satisfaction*). I work for the Downs Company myself—bookkeeper——

GAYNOR. Miss Carmody—the sick girl upstairs—she had a position there also, didn't she, before her mother died ?

NICHOLLS. Yes. She had a job as stenographer for a time. When she graduated from the business college course—I was already working at the Downs —and through my father's influence—you understand. (*Gaynor nods curtly.*) She was getting on finely, too, and liked the work. It's too bad—her mother's death, I mean—forcing her to give it up and come home to take care of those kids.

GAYNOR. It's a damn shame. That's the main cause of her breakdown.

NICHOLLS (*frowning*). I've noticed she's been looking badly lately. So that's the trouble ? Well, it's all her father's fault—and her own, too, because whenever I raised a kick about his making a slave of her, she always defended him. (*With a quick glance at the Doctor—in a confidential tone.*) Between us, Carmody's as selfish as they make 'em, if you want my opinion.

GAYNOR (*with a growl*). He's a hog on two legs.

NICHOLLS (*with a gratified smile*). You bet ! (*With a patronising air.*) I hope to get Eileen away from all this as soon as—things pick up a little. (*Making haste to explain his connection with the dubious household.*) Eileen and I have gone around together for years—went to Grammar and High School together—in different classes, of course. She's really a corker—very different from the rest of the family you've seen—like her mother. She's really educated and knows a lot—used to carry off all the prizes at school. My folks like her awfully well. Of course, they'd never stand for—him.

GAYNOR. You'll excuse my curiosity—I've a good reason for it—but you and Miss Carmody are engaged, aren't you ? Carmody said you were.

NICHOLLS (*embarrassed*). Why, yes, in a way—but nothing definite—no official announcement or anything of that kind. It's all in the future. We have to wait, you know. (*With a sentimental smile.*) We've been sort of engaged for years, you might say. It's always been sort of understood between us. (*He laughs awkwardly.*)

GAYNOR (*gravely*). Then I can be frank with you. I'd like to be because I may need your help. I don't put much faith in any promise Carmody makes. Besides, you're bound to know anyway. She'd tell you.

NICHOLLS (*a look of apprehension coming over his face*). Is it—about her sickness?

GAYNOR. Yes.

NICHOLLS. Then—it's serious?

GAYNOR. It's pulmonary tuberculosis — consumption.

NICHOLLS (*stunned*). Consumption? Good heavens! (*After a dazed pause—lamely.*) Are you sure, Doctor?

GAYNOR. Positive. (*Nicholls stares at him with vaguely frightened eyes.*) It's had a good start—thanks to her father's blind selfishness—but let's hope that can be overcome. The important thing is to ship her off to a sanatorium immediately. Carmody wouldn't hear of it at first. However, I managed to bully him into consenting; but I don't trust his word. That's where you can be of help. It's up to you to convince him that it's imperative she be sent away at once—for the safety of those around her as well as her own.

NICHOLLS (*confusedly*). I'll do my best, Doctor. (*As if he couldn't yet believe his ears—shuddering.*) Good heavens! She never said a word about—being so ill. She's had a cold. But, Doctor—do you think this sanatorium will——?

GAYNOR (*with hearty hopefulness*). Most certainly. She has every chance. The Hill Farm has a really surprising record of arrested cases—as good as any place in the country. Of course, she'll never be able to live as carelessly as before, even after the most favourable results. She'll have to take care of herself. (*Apologetically.*) I'm telling you all this as being the one most intimately concerned. I don't count Carmody. You are the one who will have to assume responsibility for her welfare when she returns to everyday life.

NICHOLLS (*answering as if he were merely talking to screen the thoughts in his mind*). Yes—certainly. Where is this sanatorium, Doctor—very far away?

GAYNOR. Half an hour by train to the town. The sanatorium is two miles out on the hills—a nice drive. You'll be able to see her whenever you've a day off. It's a pleasant trip.

NICHOLLS (*a look of horrified realisation has been creeping into his eyes*). You said—Eileen ought to be sent away—for the sake of those around her——?

GAYNOR. That's obvious. T.B. is extremely contagious, you must know that. Yet I'll bet she's been fondling and kissing those brothers and sisters of hers regardless. (*Nicholls fidgets uneasily on his chair.*)

24

And look at this house sealed tight against the fresh air! Not a window open an inch! (*Fuming.*) That's what we're up against in the fight with T.B.—a total ignorance of the commonest methods of prevention——

NICHOLLS (*his eyes shiftily avoiding the doctor's face*). Then the kids might have gotten it—by kissing Eileen?

GAYNOR. It stands to reason that's a common means of communication.

NICHOLLS (*very much shaken*). Yes. I suppose it must be. But that's terrible, isn't it? (*With sudden volubility, evidently extremely anxious to wind up this conversation and conceal his thoughts from Gaynor.*) I'll promise you, Doctor, I'll tell Carmody straight what's what. He'll pay attention to me or I'll know the reason why.

GAYNOR (*getting to his feet and picking up his overcoat*). Good boy! You've probably saved me a disagreeable squabble. I won't wait for Carmody. The sight of him makes me lose my temper. Tell him I'll be back to-morrow with definite information about the sanatorium.

NICHOLLS (*helping him on with his overcoat, anxious to have him go*). All right, Doctor.

GAYNOR (*puts on his hat*). And do your best to cheer the patient up when you talk to her. Give her confidence in her ability to get well. That's half the battle. And she'll believe it, coming from you.

NICHOLLS (*hastily*). Yes, yes, I'll do all I can.

GAYNOR (*turns to the door and shakes Nicholls' hand*

sympathetically). And don't take it to heart too much —yourself. There's every hope, remember that. In six months she'll come back to you her old self again.

NICHOLLS (*nervously*). It's hard on a fellow—so suddenly—but I'll remember—and—(*abruptly*). Good night, Doctor.

GAYNOR. Good night.

> (*He goes out. The outer door is heard shutting behind him. Nicholls closes the door, rear, and comes back and sits in the chair in front of table. He rests his chin on his hands and stares before him, a look of desperate, frightened calculation coming into his eyes. Carmody is heard clumping heavily down the stairs. A moment later he enters. His expression is glum and irritated.*)

CARMODY (*coming forward to his chair by the stove*). Has he gone away?

NICHOLLS (*turning on him with a look of repulsion*). Yes. He told me to tell you he'd be back to-morrow with definite information—about the sanatorium business.

CARMODY (*darkly*). Oho, he did, did he? Maybe I'll surprise him. I'm thinkin' it's lyin' he is about Eileen's sickness, and her lookin' as fresh as a daisy with the high colour in her cheeks when I saw her now.

NICHOLLS (*impatiently*). That's silly, Mr. Carmody. Gaynor knows his business. (*After a moment's hesitation.*) He told me all about Eileen's sickness.

CARMODY (*resentfully*). Did he now, the auld

26

monkey! Small thanks to him to be tellin' our secrets to the town.

NICHOLLS (*exasperated*). I didn't want to learn your affairs. He only told me because you'd said I and Eileen were engaged You're the one who was telling—secrets.

CARMODY (*irritated*). Ara, don't be talkin'! That's no secret at all with the whole town watchin' Eileen and you spoonin' together from the time you was kids.

NICHOLLS (*vindictively*). Well, the whole town is liable to find out—— (*He checks himself.*)

CARMODY (*too absorbed in his own troubles to notice this threat*). To hell with the town and all in it! I've troubles enough of my own. So he told you he'd send Eileen away to the hospital? I've half a mind not to let him—and let him try to make me! (*With a frown.*) But Eileen herself says she's wantin' to go, now. (*Angrily.*) It's all that divil's notion he put in her head that the children'd be catchin' her sickness that makes her willin' to go.

NICHOLLS (*with a superior air*). From what he told me, I should say it was the only thing for Eileen to do if she wants to get well quickly. (*Spitefully.*) And I'd certainly not go against Gaynor, if I was you. He told me he'd make it hot for you if you did. He will, too, you can bet on that. He's that kind.

CARMODY (*worriedly*). He's a divil. But what can he do—him and his Sasiety? I'm her father.

NICHOLLS (*seeing Carmody's uneasiness, with revengeful satisfaction*). Oh, he'll do what he says, don't worry!

27

You'll make a mistake if you think he's bluffing. It'd probably get in all the papers about you refusing. Every one would be down on you. (*As a last jab— spitefully.*) You might even lose your job over it, people would be so sore.

CARMODY (*jumping to his feet*). Ah, divil take him! Let him send her where he wants, then. I'll not be sayin' a word.

NICHOLLS (*as an afterthought*). And, honestly, Mr. Carmody, I don't see how you can object for a second —after he's told you it's absolutely necessary for Eileen to go away. (*Seeing Carmody's shaken condition, he finishes boldly.*) You've some feeling for your own daughter, haven't you? You'd be a fine father if you hadn't!

CARMODY (*apprehensively*). Whisht! She might hear you. But you're right. Let her do what she's wishful to, *and* get well soon.

NICHOLLS (*complacently—feeling his duty in the matter well done*). That's the right spirit. I knew you'd see it that way. And you and I'll do all we can to help her. (*He gets to his feet.*) Well, I guess I'll have to go. Tell Eileen——

CARMODY. You're not goin'? Sure, Eileen is puttin' on her clothes to come down and have a look at you. She'll be here in a jiffy. Sit down now, and wait for her.

NICHOLLS (*suddenly panic-stricken by the prospect of facing her*). No—no—I can't stay—I only came for a moment—I've got an appointment—honestly.

28

Besides, it isn't right for her to be up. She's too weak: It'll make her worse. You should have told her.

> (*The door in the rear is opened and Eileen enters. She is just over eighteen. Her wavy mass of dark hair is parted in the middle and combed low on her forehead, covering her ears, to a knot at the back of her head. The oval of her face is spoiled by a long, rather heavy Irish jaw contrasting with the delicacy of her other features. Her eyes are large and blue, confident in their compelling candour and sweetness; her lips, full and red, half-open over strong, even teeth, droop at the corners into an expression of wistful sadness; her clear complexion is unnaturally striking in its contrasting colours, rose and white; her figure is slight and undeveloped. She wears a plain black dress with a bit of white at the neck and wrists. She stands looking appealingly at Nicholls, who avoids her glance. Her eyes have a startled, stunned expression as if the doctor's verdict were still in her ears.*)*

EILEEN (*faintly—forcing a smile*). Good evening, Fred. (*Her eyes search his face anxiously.*)

NICHOLLS (*confusedly*). Hello, Eileen. I'm so sorry to—— (*Clumsily trying to cover up his confusion, he goes over and leads her to a chair.*) You must sit down. You've got to take care of yourself. You never ought to have got up to-night.

29

EILEEN (*sits down*). I wanted to talk to you. (*She raises her face with a pitiful smile. Nicholls hurriedly moves back to his own chair.*)

NICHOLLS (*almost brusquely*). I could have talked to you from the hall. You're silly to take chances just now.

(*Eileen's eyes show her hurt at his tone.*)

CARMODY (*seeing his chance—hastily*). You'll be stayin' a while now, Fred ? I'll take a walk down the road. I'm needin' a drink to clear my wits. (*He goes to the door in rear.*)

EILEEN (*reproachfully*). You won't be long, Father ? And please don't—you know.

CARMODY (*exasperated*). Sure who wouldn't get drunk with all the sorrows of the world piled on him ? (*He stamps out. A moment later the outside door bangs behind him. Eileen sighs. Nicholls walks up and down with his eyes on the floor.*)

NICHOLLS (*furious at Carmody for having left him in this situation.*) Honestly, Eileen, your father is the limit. I don't see how you stand for him. He's the most selfish——

EILEEN (*gently*). Sssh ! You mustn't, Fred. He's not to blame. He just doesn't understand. (*Nicholls snorts disdainfully.*) Don't ! Let's not talk about him now. We won't have many more evenings together for a long, long time. Did father or the Doctor tell you—— (*She falters.*)

NICHOLLS (*not looking at her—glumly*). Everything there was to tell, I guess.

30

EILEEN (*hastening to comfort him*). You mustn't worry, Fred. Please don't! It'd make it so much worse for me if I thought you did. I'll be all right. I'll do exactly what they tell me, and in a few months I'll be back so fat and healthy you won't know me.

NICHOLLS (*lamely*). Oh, there's no doubt of that. No one's worrying about your not getting well quick.

EILEEN. It won't be long. We can write often, and it isn't far away. You can come out and see me every Sunday—if you want to.

NICHOLLS (*hastily*). Of course I will!

EILEEN (*looking at his face searchingly*). Why do you act so funny? Why don't you sit down—here, by me? Don't you want to?

NICHOLLS (*drawing up a chair by hers—flushing guiltily*). I—I'm all flustered, Eileen. I don't know what I'm doing.

EILEEN (*putting her hand on his knee*). Poor Fred! I'm so sorry I have to go. I didn't want to at first. I knew how hard it would be on father and the kids— especially little Mary. (*Her voice trembles a bit.*) And then the doctor said if I stayed I'd be putting them all in danger. He even ordered me not to kiss them any more. (*She bites her lip to restrain a sob— then coughs, a soft, husky cough. Nicholls shrinks away from her to the edge of his chair, his eyes shifting nervously with fright. Eileen continues gently.*) So I've got to go and get well, don't you see?

NICHOLLS (*wetting his dry lips*). Yes—it's better.

EILEEN (*sadly*). I'll miss the kids so much. Taking

31

care of them has meant so much to me since mother died.' (*With a half-sob she suddenly throws her arms about his neck and hides her face on his shoulder. He shudders and fights against an impulse to push her away.*) But I'll miss you most of all, Fred. . (*She lifts her lips towards his, expecting a kiss. He seems about to kiss her —then averts his face with a shrinking movement, pretending he hasn't seen. Eileen's eyes grow wide with horror. She throws herself back into her chair, staring accusingly at Nicholls. She speaks chokingly.*) Fred! Why—why didn't you kiss—what is it ? Are you— afraid ? (*With a moaning sound.*) Oooh!

NICHOLLS (*goaded by this accusation into a display of manhood, seizes her fiercely by the arms.*) No! What—what d'you mean ? (*He tries to kiss her, but she hides her face.*)

EILEEN (*in a muffled voice of hysterical self-accusation, pushing his head away*). No, no, you mustn't! I was wrong. The doctor told you not to, didn't he ? Please don't, Fred! It would be awful if anything happened to you—through me. (*Nicholls gives up his attempts, recalled to caution by her words. She raises her face and tries to force a smile through her tears.*) But you can kiss me on the forehead, Fred. That can't do any harm. (*His face crimson, he does so. She laughs hysterically.*) It seems so silly—being kissed that way—by you. (*She gulps back a sob and continued to attempt to joke.*) I'll have to get used to it, won't I ?

THE CURTAIN FALLS

Act One : Scene Two.

The reception room of the Infirmary, a large, high-ceilinged room painted white, with oiled, hard wood floor. In the left wall, forward, a row of four windows. Farther back, the main entrance from the drive, and another window. In the rear wall left, a glass partition looking out on the sleeping porch. A row of white beds, with the faces of patients barely peeping out from under piles of heavy bed-clothes, can be seen. To the right of this partition, a bookcase, and a door leading to the hall past the patients' rooms. Farther right, another door opening on the examining room. In the right wall, rear, a door to the office. Farther forward, a row of windows. In front of the windows, a long dining-table with chairs. On the left of the table, towards the centre of the room, a chimney with two open fire-places, facing left and right. Several wicker armchairs are placed around the fire-place on the left in which a cheerful wood fire is crackling. To the left of centre, a round reading and writing table with a green-shaded electric lamp. Other electric lights are in brackets around the walls. Easy chairs stand near the table, which

33

is stacked with magazines. Rocking chairs are placed here and there about the room, near the windows, etc. A gramophone stands near the left wall, forward.

It is nearing eight o'clock of a cold evening about a week later.

At the rise of the curtain Stephen Murray is discovered sitting in a chair in front of the fireplace, left. Murray is thirty years old—a tall, slender, rather unusual-looking fellow with a pale face, sunken under high cheek bones, lined about the eyes and mouth, jaded and worn for one still so young. His intelligent, large hazel eyes have a tired, dispirited expression in repose, but can quicken instantly with a concealed mechanism of mocking, careless humour whenever his inner privacy is threatened. His large mouth aids this process of protection by a quick change from its set apathy to a cheerful grin of cynical good nature. He gives off the impression of being somehow dissatisfied with himself, but not yet embittered enough by it to take it out on others. His manner, as revealed by his speech—nervous, inquisitive, alert —seems more an acquired quality than any part of his real nature. He stoops a trifle, giving him a slightly round-shouldered appearance. He is dressed in a shabby dark suit, baggy at the knees. He is staring into the fire, dreaming, an open book lying unheeded on the arm of his chair. The gramophone is whining out the last strains of Dvorak's Humoresque. In the doorway to the office, Miss Gilpin stands talking to Miss Howard. The former *is a slight, middle-aged woman with black hair, and a strong, intelligent face, its expression of resolute efficiency softened and made kindly by her warm, sympathetic grey eyes. Miss Howard is tall, slender and blonde—decidedly pretty and provokingly conscious of it, yet with a certain air of seriousness underlying her apparent frivolity. She is twenty years old. The elder woman is dressed in the all-white of a full-fledged nurse. Miss Howard wears the grey-blue uniform of one still in training. The record finishes. Murray sighs with relief, but makes no move to get up and stop the grinding needle. Miss Howard hurries across to the machine. Miss Gilpin goes back into the office.*

MISS HOWARD (*takes off the record, glancing at Murray with amused vexation.*) It's a wonder you wouldn't stop this machine grinding itself to bits, Mr. Murray.

MURRAY (*with a smile.*) I was hoping the darn thing would bust. (*Miss Howard sniffs. Murray grins at her teasingly.*) It keeps you from talking to me. That's the real music.

MISS HOWARD (*comes over to his chair laughing*). It's easy to see you've got Irish in you. Do you know what I think? I think you're a natural born kidder. All newspaper reporters are like that, I've heard.

MURRAY. You wrong me terribly. (*Then frowning.*) And it isn't charitable to remind me of my job. I hoped to forget all about it up here.

MISS HOWARD (*surprised*). I think it's great to be

35

able to write. I wish I could. You ought to be proud of it.

MURRAY (*glumly*). I'm not. You can't call it writing—not what I did—small town stuff. (*Changing the subject.*) But I wanted to ask you something. Do you know when I'm to be moved away to the huts?

MISS HOWARD. In a few days, I guess. Don't be impatient. (*Murray grunts and moves nervously on his chair.*) What's the matter? Don't you like us here at the Sanatorium?

MURRAY (*smiling*). Oh — you — yes! (*Then seriously.*) I don't care for the atmosphere, though. (*He waves his hand towards the partition looking out on the porch.*) All those people in bed out there on the porch seem so sick. It's depressing. I can't do anything for them—and—it makes me feel so helpless.

MISS HOWARD. Well, it's the rules, you know. All the patients have to come here first until Doctor Stanton finds out whether they're well enough to be sent out to the huts and cottages. And remember you're a patient just like the ones in bed out there— even if you are up and about.

MURRAY. I know it. But I don't feel as I were —really sick like them.

MISS HOWARD (*wisely*). None of them do, either.

MURRAY (*after a moment's reflection—cynically*). Yes, I suppose it's that pipe dream that keeps us all going, eh?

36

MISS HOWARD. Well, you ought to be thankful. You're very lucky, if you knew it. (*Lowering her voice.*) Shall I tell you a secret? I've seen your chart and *you've* no cause to worry. Doctor Stanton joked about it. He said you were too uninteresting —there was so little the matter with you.

MURRAY (*pleased, but pretending indifference*). Humph! He's original in that opinion.

MISS HOWARD. I know it's hard your being the only one up the week since you've been here, with no one to talk to; but there's another patient due to-day. Maybe she'll be well enough to be around with you. (*With a quick glance at her wrist watch.*) She can't be coming unless she got in on the last train.

MURRAY (*interestedly*). It's a she, eh?

MISS HOWARD. Yes.

MURRAY (*grinning provokingly*). Young?

MISS HOWARD. Eighteen, I believe. (*Seeing his grin—with feigned pique.*) I suppose you'll be asking if she's pretty next! Oh, you men are all alike, sick or well. Her name is Carmody, that's the only other thing I know. So there!

MURRAY. Carmody?

MISS HOWARD. Oh, you don't know her. She's from another part of the state from your town.

MISS GILPIN (*appearing in the office doorway*). Miss Howard.

MISS HOWARD. Yes, Miss Gilpin. (*In an aside to*

37

Murray as she leaves him.)   It's time for those horrid
diets.

> (*She hurries back into the office. Murray
> stares into the fire. Miss Howard re-
> appears from the office and goes out by
> the door to the hall, rear. Carriage
> wheels are heard from the drive in
> front of the house on the left. They stop.
> After a pause there is a sharp rap on the
> door and a bell rings insistently. Men's
> muffled voices are heard in argument.
> Murray turns curiously in his chair.
> Miss Gilpin comes from the office and
> walks quickly to the door, unlocking and
> opening it. Eileen enters, followed by
> Nicholls, who is carrying her suit-case,
> and by her father.*)

EILEEN. I'm Miss Carmody. I believe Doctor
Gaynor wrote——

MISS GILPIN (*taking her hand—with kind affability*).
We've been expecting you all day. How do you
do ? I'm Miss Gilpin. You came on the last
train, didn't you ?

EILEEN (*heartened by the other woman's kindness*).
Yes. This is my father, Miss Gilpin—and Mr.
Nicholls.

> (*Miss Gilpin shakes hands cordially with the
> two men who are staring about the room
> in embarrassment. Carmody has very
> evidently been drinking. His voice is
> thick and his face puffed and stupid.*)

Nicholls' manner is that of one who is accomplishing a necessary but disagreeable duty with the best grace possible, but is frightfully eager to get it over and done with. Carmody's condition embarrasses him acutely and when he glances at him it is with hatred and angry disgust.)

MISS GILPIN (*indicating the chairs in front of the windows on the left, forward*). Won't you gentlemen sit down? (*Carmody grunts sullenly and plumps himself into the one nearest the door. Nicholls hesitates, glancing down at the suit-case he carries. Miss Gilpin turns to Eileen.*) And now we'll get you settled immediately. Your room is all ready for you. If you'll follow me—— (*She turns toward the door in rear, centre.*)

EILEEN. Let me take the suit-case now, Fred.

MISS GILPIN (*as he is about to hand it to her—decisively*). No, my dear, you mustn't. Put the case right down there, Mr. Nicholls. I'll have it taken to Miss Carmody's room in a moment. (*She shakes her finger at Eileen with kindly admonition.*) That's the first rule you'll have to learn. Never exert yourself or tax your strength. It's very important. You'll find laziness is a virtue instead of a vice with us.

EILEEN (*confused*). I—— I didn't know——

MISS GILPIN (*smiling*). Of course you didn't. And now if you'll come with me I'll show you your room. We'll have a little chat there and I can explain

39

all the other important rules in a second. The gentlemen can make themselves comfortable in the meantime. We won't be gone more than a moment.

NICHOLLS (*feeling called upon to say something*). Yes—we'll wait—certainly, we're all right.

> (*Carmody remains silent, glowering at the fire. Nicholls sits down beside him. Miss Gilpin and Eileen go out. Murray switches his chair so that he can observe the two men out of the corner of his eye while pretending to be absorbed in his book.*)

CARMODY (*looking about shiftily and reaching for the inside pocket of his overcoat*). I'll be havin' a nip now we're alone, and that cacklin' hen gone. I'm feelin' sick in the pit of the stomach. (*He pulls out a pint flask, half full.*)

NICHOLLS (*excitedly*). For God's sake, don't! Put that bottle away! (*In a whisper.*) Don't you see that fellow in the chair there?

CARMODY (*taking a big drink*). Ah, I'm not mindin' a man at all. Sure I'll bet it's himself would be likin' a taste of the same. (*He appears about to get up and invite Murray to join him, but Nicholls grabs his arm.*)

NICHOLLS (*with a frightened look at Murray who appears buried in his book*). Stop it, you—— Don't you know he's probably a patient and they don't allow them——

CARMODY (*scornfully*). A sick one, and him readin' a book like a dead man without a civil word out of

40

him! It's queer they'd be allowin' the sick ones to read books, when I'll bet it's the same lazy readin' in the house brought the half of them down with the consumption itself. (*Raising his voice.*) I'm thinking this whole shebang is a big, thievin' fake—and I've always thought so.

NICHOLLS (*furiously*). Put that bottle away, damn it! And don't shout. You're not in a public-house.

CARMODY (*with provoking calm*). I'll put it back when I'm ready, not before, and no lip from you!

NICHOLLS (*with fierce disgust*). You're drunk now. It's disgusting.

CARMODY (*raging*). Drunk, am I? Is it the like of a young jackass like you that's still wet behind the ears to be tellin' me I'm drunk?

NICHOLLS (*half-rising from his chair—pleadingly*). For heaven's sake, Mr. Carmody, remember where we are and don't raise any rumpus. What'll Eileen say? Do you want to make trouble for her at the start?

CARMODY (*puts the bottle away hastily, mumbling to himself—then glowers about the room scornfully with blinking eyes*). It's a grand hotel this is, I'm thinkin', for the rich to be takin' their ease, and not a hospital for the poor, but the poor has to pay for it.

NICHOLLS (*fearful of another outbreak*). Sssh!

CARMODY. Don't be shshin' at me? I'm tellin' you the truth. I'd make Eileen come back out of this to-night if that divil of a doctor didn't have me by the throat.

41

NICHOLLS (*glancing at him nervously*). I wonder how soon she'll be back ? The carriage is waiting for us. We'll have to hurry to make that last train back. If we miss it—it means two hours on the damn tram.

CARMODY (*angrily*). Is it anxious to get out of her sight you are, and you engaged to marry and pretendin' to love her ? (*Nicholls flushes guiltily. Murray pricks up his ears and stares over at Nicholls. The latter meets his glance, scowls, and hurriedly averts his eyes. Carmody goes on accusingly.*) Sure, it's no heart at all you have—and her your sweetheart for years—and her sick with the consumption—and you wild to run away from her and leave her alone.

NICHOLLS (*springing to his feet—furiously*). That's a——! (*He controls himself with an effort. His voice trembles.*) You're not responsible for the idiotic things you're saying or I'd——. (*He turns away, seeking some escape from the old man's tongue.*) I'll see if the man is still there with the carriage. (*He walks to the door on left and goes out.*)

CARMODY (*following him with his eyes*). Go to hell, for all I'm preventin' You've got no guts of a man in you. (*He addresses Murray with the good nature inspired by the flight of Nicholls.*) Is it true you're one of the consumptives, young fellow ?

MURRAY (*delighted by this speech—with a grin*). Yes, I'm one of them.

CARMODY. My name's Carmody. What's yours, then ?

MURRAY. Murray.

CARMODY (*slapping his thigh*). Irish as Paddy's pig! (*Murray nods. Carmody brightens and grows confidential.*) I'm glad to be knowin' you're one of us. You can keep an eye on Eileen. That's my daughter that came with us. She's got consumption like yourself.

MURRAY. I'll be glad to do all I can.

CARMODY. Thanks to you—though it's a grand life she'll be havin' here from the fine look of the place. (*With whining self-pity.*) It's me it's hard on, God help me, with four small children and me widowed, and havin' to hire a woman to come in and look after them and the house now that Eileen's sick; and payin' for her curin' in this place, and me with only a bit of money in the bank for my old age. That's hard, now, on a man, and who'll say it isn't?

MURRAY (*made uncomfortable by this confidence*). Hard luck always comes in bunches. (*To head off Carmody who is about to give vent to more woe—quickly, with a glance towards the door from the hall.*) If I'm not mistaken, here comes your daughter now.

CARMODY (*as Eileen comes into the room*). I'll make you acquainted. Eileen! (*She comes over to them, embarrassed to find her father in his condition so chummy with a stranger. Murray rises to his feet.*) This is Mr. Murray, Eileen. I want you to meet. He's Irish and he'll put you on to the ropes of the place. He's got the consumption, too, God pity him.

EILEEN (*distressed*). Oh, Father, how can you—— (*With a look at Murray which pleads for her father.*) I'm glad to meet you, Mr. Murray.

43

MURRAY (*with a straight glance at her which is so frankly admiring that she flushes and drops her eyes.*) I'm glad to meet you. (*The front door is opened and Nicholls re-appears, shivering with the cold. He stares over at the others with ill-concealed irritation.*)

CARMODY (*noticing him—with malicious satisfaction*). Oho, here you are again. (*Nicholls scowls and turns away. Carmody addresses his daughter with a sly wink at Murray.*) I thought Fred was slidin' down hill to the train with his head bare to the frost, and him so desperate hurried to get away from here. Look at the knees on him clappin' together with the cold, and with the great fear that's in him he'll be catchin' a sickness in this place! (*Nicholls, his guilty conscience stabbed to the quick, turns pale with impotent rage.*)

EILEEN (*remonstrating pitifully*). Father! Please! (*She hurries over to Nicholls.*) Oh, please don't mind him, Fred. You know what he is when he's drinking. He doesn't mean a word he's saying.

NICHOLLS (*thickly*). That's all right—for you to say. But I won't forget—I'm sick and tired standing for—I'm not used to—such people.

EILEEN (*shrinking from him*). Fred!

NICHOLLS (*with a furious glance at Murray*). Before that cheap slob, too—letting him know everything!

EILEEN (*faintly*). He seems—very nice.

NICHOLLS. You've got your eyes set on him already, have you? Leave it to you! No fear of your not having a good time of it out here!

EILEEN. Fred!

NICHOLLS. Well, go ahead if you want to. I don't care. I'll—— (*Startled by the look of anguish which comes over her face, he hastily swallows his words. He takes out his watch—fiercely.*) We'll miss that train, damn it!

EILEEN (*in a stricken tone*). Oh, Fred! (*Then forcing back her tears she calls to Carmody in a strained voice.*) Father! You'll have to go now. Miss Gilpin told me to tell you you'd have to go right away to catch the train.

CARMODY (*shaking hands with Murray*). I'll be goin'. Keep your eye on her. I'll be out soon to see her and you and me'll have another talk.

MURRAY. Glad to. Good-bye for the present. (*He walks to windows on the far right, turning his back considerately on their leave-taking.*)

EILEEN (*comes to Carmody and hangs on his arm as they proceed to the door*). Be sure and kiss them all for me—Billy and Tom and Nora and little Mary— and bring them out to see me as soon as you can, father, please! And you come often, too, won't you? And don't forget to tell Mrs. Brennan all the directions I gave you coming out on the train. I told her, but she mightn't remember—about Mary's bath—and to give Tom his——

CARMODY (*impatiently*). Hasn't she brought up brats of her own, and doesn't she know the way of it? Don't be worryin' now, like a fool.

EILEEN (*helplessly*). Never mind telling her, then. I'll write to her.

CARMODY. You'd better not. Leave her alone. She'll not wish you mixin' in with her work and tellin' her how to do it.

EILEEN (*aghast*). *Her* work ! (*She seems at the end of her tether—wrung too dry for any further emotion. She kisses her father at the door with indifference and speaks calmly.*) Good-bye, father.

CARMODY (*in a whining tone of injury*). A cold kiss ! And never a small tear out of her ! Is your heart a stone ? (*Drunken tears well from his eyes and he blubbers.*) And your own father going back to a lone house with a stranger in it !

EILEEN (*wearily, in a dead voice*). You'll miss your train, father.

CARMODY (*raging in a second*). I'm off, then ! Come on, Fred. It's no welcome we have with her here in this place—and a great curse on this day I brought her to it ! (*He stamps out.*)

EILEEN (*in the same dead tone*). Good-bye, Fred.

NICHOLLS (*repenting his words of a moment ago— confusedly*). I'm sorry, Eileen—for what I said. I didn't mean—you know what your father is—excuse me, won't you ?

EILEEN (*without feeling*). Yes.

NICHOLLS. And I'll be out soon—in a week if I can make it. Well then,—good-bye for the present. (*He bends down as if to kiss her, but she shrinks back out of his reach.*)

EILEEN (*a faint trace of mockery in her weary voice*). No, Fred. Remember you mustn't now.

NICHOLLS (*in an instant huff*). Oh, if that's the way you feel about——

> (*He strides out and slams the door viciously behind him. Eileen walks slowly back towards the fire-place, her face fixed in a dead calm of despair. As she sinks into one of the armchairs, the strain becomes too much. She breaks down, hiding her face in her hands, her frail shoulders heaving with the violence of her sobs. At this sound, Murray turns from the windows and comes over near her chair.*)

MURRAY (*after watching her for a moment—in an embarrassed tone of sympathy*). Come on, Miss Carmody, that'll never do. I know it's hard at first —but—getting yourself all worked up is bad for you. You'll run a temperature and then they'll keep you in bed—which isn't pleasant. Take hold of yourself! It isn't so bad up here—really—once you get used to it! (*The shame she feels at giving way in the presence of a stranger only adds to her loss of control and she sobs heartbrokenly. Murray walks up and down nervously, visibly nonplussed and upset. Finally he hits upon something.*) One of the nurses will be in any minute. You don't want them to see you like this.

EILEEN (*chokes back her sobs and finally raises her face and attempts a smile*). I'm sorry—to make such a sight of myself. I just couldn't help it.

MURRAY (*jocularly*). Well, they say a good cry does you a lot of good.

47

EILEEN (*forcing a smile*). I do feel—better.

MURRAY (*staring at her with a quizzical smile—cynically*). You shouldn't take those lovers' squabbles so seriously. To-morrow he'll be sorry—you'll be sorry. He'll write begging forgiveness—you'll do ditto. Result—all serene again.

EILEEN (*a shadow of pain on her face—with dignity*). Don't—please.

MURRAY (*angry at himself—hanging his head contritely*). I'm a fool. Pardon me. I'm rude sometimes—before I know it. (*He shakes off his confusion with a renewed attempt at a joking tone.*) You can blame your father for any breaks I make. He made me your guardian, you know—told me to see that you behaved.

EILEEN (*with a genuine smile*). Oh, father! (*Flushing.*) You mustn't mind anything he said to-night.

MURRAY (*thoughtlessly*). Yes, he was well lit up. I envied him. (*Eileen looks very shame-faced. Murray sees it and exclaims in exasperation at himself.*) Darn! There I go again putting my foot in it! (*With an irrepressible grin.*) I ought to have my tongue operated on—that's what's the matter with me. (*He laughs and throws himself in a chair.*)

EILEEN (*forced in spite of herself to smile with him*). You're candid, at any rate, Mr. Murray.

MURRAY. Don't misunderstand me. Far be it from me to cast slurs at your father's high spirits. I said I envied him his jag and that's the truth. The

48

same candour compels me to confess that I was pickled to the gills myself when I arrived here. Fact! I made love to all the nurses and generally disgraced myself—and had a wonderful time.

EILEEN. I suppose it does make you forget your troubles—for a while.

MURRAY (*waving this aside*). I didn't want to forget—not for a second. I wasn't drowning my sorrow. I was hilariously celebrating.

EILEEN (*astonished—by this time quite interested in this queer fellow to the momentary forgetfulness of her own grief*). Celebrating—coming here? But—aren't you sick?

MURRAY. T. B.? Yes, of course. (*Confidentially.*) But it's only a matter of time when I'll be all right again. I hope it won't be too soon. I was dying for a rest—a good, long rest with time to think about things. I'm due to get what I wanted here. That's why I celebrated.

EILEEN (*with wide eyes*). I wonder if you really mean——

MURRAY. What I've been sayin'? I sure do—every word of it!

EILEEN (*puzzled*). I can't understand how anyone could—— (*With a worried glance over her shoulder.*) I think I'd better look for Miss Gilpin, hadn't I? She may wonder—— (*She half rises from her chair.*)

MURRAY (*quickly*). No. Please don't go yet. Sit down. Please do. (*She glances at him irresolutely,*

49

then resumes her chair.) They'll give you your diet of milk and shoo you off to bed on that freezing porch soon enough, don't worry. I'll see to it that you don't fracture any rules. (*Hitching his chair nearer hers—impulsively.*) In all charity to me you've got to stick awhile. I haven't had a chance to really talk to a soul for a week. You found what I said a while ago hard to believe, didn't you ?

EILEEN (*with a smile*). Isn't it ? You said you hoped you wouldn't get well too soon !

MURRAY. And I meant it ! This place is honestly like heaven to me—a lonely heaven till your arrival. (*Eileen looks embarrassed.*) And why wouldn't it be ? I've no fear for my health—eventually. Just let me tell you what I was getting away from—— (*With a sudden laugh full of a weary bitterness.*) Do you know what it means to work from seven at night till three in the morning as a reporter on a morning newspaper in a town of twenty thousand people—for *ten years ?* No. You don't. You can't. No one could who hadn't been through the mill. But what it did to me—it made me happy—yes, happy !—to get out here—T. B. and all, notwithstanding.

EILEEN (*looking at him curiously*). But I always thought being a reporter was so interesting.

MURRAY (*with a cynical laugh*). Interesting ? On a small town rag ? A month of it, perhaps, when you're a kid and new to the game. But ten years. Think of it ! With only a raise of a couple of dollars every blue moon or so, and a weekly spree on Saturday night to vary the monotony. (*He laughs again.*)

50

Interesting, eh? Getting the dope on the Social of the Queen Esther Circle in the basement of the Methodist Episcopal Church, unable to sleep through a meeting of the Common Council on account of the noisy oratory caused by John Smith's application for a permit to build a house; making a note that a tugboat towed two barges loaded with coal up the river, that Mrs. Perkins spent a week-end with relatives in Hickville, that John Jones—— Oh help! Why go on? Ten years of it! I'm a broken man. God, how I used to pray that our Congressman would commit suicide, or the Mayor murder his wife— just to be able to write a real story!

EILEEN (*with a smile*). Is it as bad as that? But weren't there other things in the town—outside your work—that were interesting?

MURRAY (*decidedly*). No Never anything new —and I knew everyone and every thing in town by heart years ago (*With sudden bitterness.*) Oh, it was my own fault Why didn't I get out of it? Well, I didn't. I was always going to—to-morrow— and to-morrow never came. I got in a rut—and stayed put. People seem to get that way, somehow —in that town. It's in the air. All the boys I grew up with—nearly all, at least—took root in the same way. It took pleurisy, followed by T. B., to blast me loose.

EILEEN (*wonderingly*). But — your family — didn't they live there?

MURRAY. I haven't much of a family left. My mother died when I was a kid. My father—he was a lawyer—died when I was nineteen, just about to go to college. He left nothing, so I went to work on the paper instead. And there I've been ever since. I've two sisters, respectably married and living in another part of the state. We don't get along—but they are paying for me here, so I suppose I've no kick. (*Cynically.*) A family wouldn't have changed things. From what I've seen that blood-thicker-than-water dope is all wrong. It's thinner than table-d'hôte soup. You may have seen a bit of that truth in your own case already.

EILEEN (*shocked*). How can you say that? You don't know——

MURRAY. Don't I, though? Wait till you've been here three months or four—when the gap you left has been comfortably filled. You'll see then!

EILEEN (*angrily, her lips trembling*). You must be crazy to say such things! (*Fighting back her tears.*) Oh, I think it's hateful—when you see how badly I feel!

MURRAY (*in acute confusion. Stammering*). Look here, Miss Carmody, I didn't mean to——. Listen—don't feel mad at me, please. My tongue ran away with me. I was only talking. I'm like that. You mustn't take it seriously.

EILEEN (*still resentful*). I don't see how you can talk. You don't—you can't know about these things —when you've just said you had no family of your own, really.

MURRAY (*eager to return to her good graces*). No.

Of course I don't know. I was just talking regardless for the fun of listening to it.

EILEEN (*after a pause*). Hasn't either of your sisters any children ?

MURRAY. One of them has—two of them—ugly, squally little brats.

EILEEN (*disapprovingly*). You don't like babies ?

MURRAY (*bluntly*). No. (*Then with a grin at her shocked face.*) I don't get them. They're something I can't seem to get acquainted with.

EILEEN (*with a smile, indulgently*). You're a funny person. (*Then with a superior, motherly air.*) No wonder you couldn't understand how badly I feel. (*With a tender smile.*) I've four of them—my brothers and sisters—though they're not what you'd call babies, except to me. Billy is fourteen, Nora eleven, Tom ten, and even little Mary is eight. I've been a mother to them now for a whole year—ever since our mother died (*Sadly.*) And I don't know how they'll ever get along while I'm away.

MURRAY (*cynically*). Oh, they'll—— (*He checks what he was going to say and adds lamely*)——get along somehow.

EILEEN (*with the same superior tone*). It's easy for you to say that. You don't know how children grow to depend on you for everything. You're not a woman.

MURRAY (*with a grin*). Are you ? (*Then with a chuckle.*) You're as old as the pyramids, aren't you ?

53

I feel like a little boy. Won't you adopt me, too ?

EILEEN (*flushing, with a shy smile*). Someone ought to. (*Quickly changing the subject.*) Do you know, I can't get over what you said about hating your work so. I should think it would be wonderful —to be able to write things.

MURRAY. My job had nothing to do with writing. To write—really write—yes, that's something worth trying for. That's what I've always meant to have a stab at. I've run across ideas enough for stories— that sounded good to me, anyway. (*With a forced laugh.*) But—like everything else—I never got down to it. I started one or two—but—either I thought I didn't have the time or—— (*He shrugs his shoulders.*)

EILEEN. Well, you've plenty of time now, haven't you ?

MURRAY (*instantly struck by this suggestion*). You mean—— I could write—up here ? (*She nods. His face lights up with enthusiasm.*) Say ! That is an idea ! Thank you ! I'd never have had sense enough to have thought of that myself. (*Eileen flushes with pleasure.*) Sure there's time—nothing but time up here——

EILEEN. Then you seriously think you'll try it ?

MURRAY (*determinedly*). Yes. Why not ? I've got to try and do something real some time, haven't I ? I've no excuse not to, now. My mind isn't sick.

EILEEN (*excitedly*). That'll be wonderful !

MURRAY (*confidently*). Listen. I've had ideas for a series of short stories for the last couple of years—small town experiences, some of them actual. I know that life—too darn well. I ought to be able to write about it. And if I can sell one—to the *Post*, say— I'm sure they'd take the others, too. And then—— I should worry! It'd be easy sailing. But you must promise to help—play critic for me—read them and tell me where they're rotten.

EILEEN (*pleased, but protesting*). Oh, no, I'd never dare. I don't know anything——

MURRAY. Yes, you do. You're the public. And you started me off on this thing—if I'm really starting at last. So you've got to back me up now. (*Suddenly.*) Say, I wonder if they'd let me have a typewriter up here?

EILEEN. It'd be fine if they would. I'd like to have one, too—to practice. I learned stenography at a business college and then I had a position for a year—before my mother died.

MURRAY. We could hire one—I could. I don't see why they wouldn't allow it. I'm to be sent to one of the men's huts within the next few days, and you'll be shipped to one of the women's cottages within ten days. You're not sick enough to be kept here in bed, I'm sure of that.

EILEEN. I—— I don't know——

MURRAY. Here! None of that! You just think you're not and you won't be. Say, I'm keen on that typewriter idea. They couldn't kick if we only used it during recreation periods. I could have it a week, and then you a week.

EILEEN (*eagerly*). And I could type your stories after you've written them! I *could* help that way.

MURRAY (*smiling*). But I'm quite able—— (*Then seeing how interested she is he adds hurriedly.*) That'd be great! It'd save so much time. I've always been a fool at a machine. And I'd be willing to pay whatever—— (*Miss Gilpin enters from the rear and walks towards them.*)

EILEEN (*quickly*). Oh, no! I'd be glad to get the practice. I wouldn't accept—— (*She coughs slightly.*)

MURRAY (*with a laugh*). Maybe, after you've read my stuff, you won't type it at any price.

MISS GILPIN. Miss Carmody, may I speak to you for a moment, please.

> (*She takes Eileen aside and talks to her in low tones of admonition. Eileen's face falls. She nods a horrified acquiescence. Miss Gilpin leaves her and goes into the office, rear.*)

MURRAY (*as Eileen comes back. Noticing her perturbation. Kindly*). Well? Now, what's the trouble?

EILEEN (*her lips trembling*). She told me I mustn't forget to shield my mouth with my handkerchief when I cough.

MURRAY (*consolingly*). Yes, that's one of the rules, you know.

56

EILEEN (*falteringly*). She said they'd give me—a —cup to carry around—— (*She stops, shuddering.*)

MURRAY (*easily*). It's not as horrible as it sounds. They're only little paste-board things you carry in your pocket.

EILEEN (*as if speaking to herself*). It's so horrible. (*She holds out her hand to Murray.*) I'm to go to my room now. Good night, Mr. Murray.

MURRAY (*holding her hand for a moment—earnestly*). Don't mind your first impressions here. You'll look on everything as a matter of course in a few days. I felt your way at first. (*He drops her hand and shakes his finger at her.*) Mind your guardian, now! (*She forces a trembling smile.*) See you at breakfast. Good night.

> (*Eileen goes out to the hall in rear. Miss Howard comes in from the door just after her, carrying a glass of milk.*)

MISS HOWARD. Almost bedtime, Mr. Murray. Here's your diet. (*He takes the glass. She smiles at him provokingly.*) Well, is it love at first sight, Mr. Murray?

MURRAY (*with a grin*). Sure thing! You can consider yourself heartlessly jilted. (*He turns and raises his glass towards the door through which Eileen has just gone, as if toasting her.*)

> "A glass of milk, and thou
> Coughing beside me in the wilderness——
> Ah——wilderness were Paradise enow!"

> (*He takes a sip of milk.*)

57

MISS HOWARD (*peevishly*). That's old stuff, Mr. Murray. A patient at Saranac wrote that parody.

MURRAY (*maliciously*). Aha, you've discovered it's a parody, have you, you sly minx! (*Miss Howard turns from him huffily and walks back towards the office, her chin in the air.*)

THE CURTAIN FALLS

The Straw
Act Two

Act Two: Scene One

*The assembly room of the main building of the sanatorium
—early in the morning of a fine day in June, four
months later. The room is large, light and airy,
painted a fresh white. On the left forward, an
armchair. Farther back, a door opening on the
main hall. To the rear of this door, a pianola on
a raised platform. At back of the pianola, a door
leading into the office. In the rear wall, a long
series of French windows looking out on the lawn,
with wooded hills in the far background. Shrubs
in flower grow immediately outside the windows.
Inside, there is a row of potted plants. In the
right wall, rear, four windows. Farther forward,
a long well-filled bookcase, and a doorway leading
into the dining-room. Following the walls, but
about five feet out from them a stiff line of chairs
placed closely against each other forms a sort of
right-angled auditorium of which the large, square
table that stands at centre, forward, would seem
to be the stage.*

*From the dining-room comes the clatter of dishes, the
confused murmur of many voices, male and female—
all the mingled sounds of a crowd of people at a meal.*

*After the curtain rises, Doctor Stanton enters
from the hall, followed by a visitor, Mr. Sloan,
and the assistant physician, Doctor Simms. Doctor
Stanton is a handsome man of forty-five or so with
a grave, care-lined, studious face lightened by a
kindly, humorous smile. His grey eyes, saddened
by the suffering they have witnessed, have the
sympathetic quality of real understanding. The
look they give is full of companionship, the courage-
renewing, human companionship of a hope which
is shared. He speaks with a slight Southern
accent, soft and slurring. Doctor Simms is a tall,
angular young man with a long sallow face and a
sheepish, self-conscious grin. Mr. Sloan is fifty,
short and stout, well dressed—one of the successful
business men whose endowments have made the
Hill Farm a possibility.*

STANTON (*as they enter*). This is what you might
call the general assembly room, Mr. Sloan—where
the patients of both sexes are allowed to congre-
gate together after meals, for diets, and in the
evening.

SLOAN (*looking around him*). Couldn't be more
pleasant, I must say—light and airy. (*He walks to
where he can take a peep into the dining-room.*) Ah,
they're all at breakfast, I see.

STANTON (*smiling*). Yes, and with no lack of
appetite, let me tell you. (*With a laugh of proud
satisfaction.*) They'd sure eat us out of house and
home at one sitting, if we'd give them the opportunity.
(*To his assistant.*) Wouldn't they, Doctor?

62

SIMMS (*with his abashed grin*). You bet they would, sir.

SLOAN (*with a smile*). That's fine. (*With a nod towards the dining-room.*) The ones in there are the sure cures, aren't they ?

STANTON (*a shadow coming over his face*). Strictly speaking, there are no sure cures in this disease, Mr. Sloan. When we permit a patient to return to take up his or her activities in the world, the patient is what we call an arrested case. The disease is overcome, quiescent ; the wound is healed over. It's then up to the patient to so take care of himself that this condition remains permanent. It isn't hard for them to do this, usually. Just ordinary, bull-headed common sense—added to what they've learned here— is enough for their safety. And the precautions we teach them to take don't diminish their social usefulness in the slightest, either, as I can prove by our statistics of former patients. (*With a smile.*) It's rather early in the morning for statistics, though.

SLOAN (*with a wave of the hand*). Oh, you needn't. Your reputation in that respect, Doctor—— (*Stanton inclines his head in acknowledgment. Sloan jerks his thumb towards the dining-room*). But the ones in there *are* getting well, aren't they ?

STANTON. To all appearances, yes. You don't dare swear to it, though. Sometimes, just when a case looks most favourably, there's a sudden, unforeseen breakdown, and they have to be sent back to bed, or, if it's very serious, back to the Infirmary again. These are the exceptions, however, not the

63

rule. You can bank on most of those eaters being out in the world and usefully employed within six months.

SLOAN. You couldn't say more than that (*Abruptly*). But—the unfortunate ones—do you have many deaths ?

STANTON (*with a frown*). No. We're under a very hard, almost cruel imperative which prevents that. If, at the end of six months, a case shows no response to treatment, continues to go down hill— if, in a word, it seems hopeless—we send them away, to one of the State Farms if they have no private means. (*Apologetically.*) You see, this sanatorium is overcrowded and has a long waiting list, most of the time, of others who demand their chance for life. We have to make places for them. We have no time to waste on incurables. There are other places for them—and sometimes, too, a change is beneficial and they pick up in new surroundings. You never can tell. But we're bound by the rule. It may seem cruel—but it's as near justice to all concerned as we can come.

SLOAN (*soberly*). I see. (*His eyes fall on the pianola —in surprise.*) Ah—a piano.

STANTON (*replying to the other's thought*). Yes, the patients play and sing. (*With a smile.*) If you'd call the noise they make by those terms. They'd dance, too, if we permitted it. There's only one song taboo—Home, Sweet Home. We forbid that —for obvious reasons.

SLOAN. I see. (*With a final look around.*) Did I

understand you to say this is the only place where the sexes are permitted to mingle?

STANTON. Yes, sir.

SLOAN (*with a smile*). Not much chance for a love affair then.

STANTON (*seriously*). We do our best to prevent them. We even have a strict rule which allows us to step in and put a stop to any intimacy which grows beyond the casual. People up here, Mr. Sloan, are expected to put aside all ideas except the one—getting well.

SLOAN (*somewhat embarrassed*). A damn good rule, too, I should say, under the circumstances.

STANTON (*with a laugh*). Yes, we're strictly anti-Cupid, sir, from top to bottom. (*Turning to the door to the hall.*) And now, if you don't mind, Mr. Sloan, I'm going to turn you loose to wander about the grounds on an unconducted tour. To-day is my busy morning—Saturday. We weigh each patient immediately after breakfast.

SLOAN. Every week?

STANTON. Every Saturday. You see we depend on fluctuations in weight to tell us a lot about the patient's condition. If they gain, or stay at normal, all's usually well. If they lose week after week without any reason we can definitely point to, we keep careful watch. It's a sign that something's wrong. We're forewarned by it and on our guard.

SLOAN (*with a smile*). Well, I'm certainly learning things. (*He turns to the door.*) And you just shoo

65

me off wherever you please and go on with the good work. I'll be glad of a ramble in the open on such a glorious morning.

STANTON. After the weighing is over, sir, I'll be free to——

> (*His words are lost as the three go out. A moment later, Eileen enters from the dining-room. She has grown stouter, her face has more of a healthy, out-of-door colour, but there is still about her the suggestion of being worn down by a burden too oppressive for her courage. She is dressed in blouse and dark skirt. She goes to the armchair, left forward, and sinks down on it. She is evidently in a state of nervous depression; she twists her fingers together in her lap; her eyes stare sadly before her; she clenches her upper lip with her teeth to prevent its trembling. She has hardly regained control over herself when Stephen Murray comes in hurriedly from the dining-room and, seeing her at his first glance, walks quickly over to her chair. He is the picture of health, his figure has filled out solidly, his tanned face beams with suppressed exultation.*)

MURRAY (*excitedly*). Eileen! I saw you leave your table. I've something to tell you. I didn't get a chance last night after the mail came. You'd gone to the cottage. Just listen, Eileen—it's too good to be true—but on that mail—guess what?

66

EILEEN (*forgetting her depression—with an excited .mile*). I know! You've sold your story!

MURRAY (*triumphantly*). Go to the head of the class. What d'you know about that for luck! My first, too—and only the third magazine I sent it to! (*He cuts a joyful caper.*)

EILEEN (*happily*). Isn't that wonderful, Stephen! But I knew all the time you would. The story's so good.

MURRAY. Well, you might have known, but I didn't think there was a chance in the world. And as for being good—— (*With superior air*)——wait till I turn loose with the real big ones, the kind I'm going to write. Then I'll make them sit up and take notice. They can't stop me now. This money gives me a chance to sit back and do what I please for a while. And I haven't told you the best part. The editor wrote saying how much he liked the yarn and asked me for more of the same kind.

EILEEN. And you've the three others about the same person—just as good, too! Why, you'll sell them all! (*She clasps her hands delightedly.*)

MURRAY. And I can send them out right away. They're all typed, thanks to you. That's what's brought me luck, I know. I never had a bit by myself. (*Then, after a quick glance around to make sure they are alone, he bends down and kisses her.*) There! A token of gratitude—even if it is against the rules.

EILEEN (*flushing—with timid happiness*). Stephen! You mustn't! They'll see.

67

MURRAY (*boldly*). Let them !

EILEEN. But you know—they've warned us against being so much together, already.

MURRAY. Let them ! We'll be out of this prison soon. (*Eileen shakes her head sadly, but he does not notice.*) Oh, I wish you could leave when I do. We'd have some celebration together.

EILEEN (*her lips trembling*). I was thinking last night—that you'd soon be going away. You look so well. Do you think—they'll let you go—soon ?

MURRAY. You bet I do. I'm bound to go now. It's ridiculous keeping me here when I'm as healthy as a pig. I caught Stanton in the hall last night and asked him if I could go.

EILEEN (*anxiously*). What did he say ?

MURRAY. He only smiled and said : " We'll see if you gain weight to-morrow." As if that mattered now ! Why, I'm way above normal as it is ! But you know Stanton—always putting you off. But I could tell by the way he said it he'd be willing to consider——

EILEEN (*slowly*). Then—if you gain to-day——

MURRAY. He'll let me go. Yes, I know he will. I'm going to insist on it.

EILEEN. Then—you'll leave——?

MURRAY. Right away. The minute I can get packed.

EILEEN (*trying to force a smile*). Oh, I'm so glad— for your sake ; but- ·I'm selfish—it'll be so lonely here without you.

68

MURRAY (*consolingly*). You'll be going away yourself before long. (*Eileen shakes her head. He goes on without noticing, wrapped in his own success.*) Oh, Eileen, you can't imagine all it opens up for me—selling that story. I don't have to go back home to stagnate. I can go straight to New York, and live, and meet real people who are doing things. I can take my time, and try and do the work I hope to. (*Feelingly.*) You don't know how grateful I am to you, Eileen—how you've helped me. Oh, I don't mean just the typing, I mean your encouragement, your faith! I'd never have had guts enough to stick to it myself. The stories would never have been written if it hadn't been for you.

EILEEN (*choking back a sob*). I didn't do—anything.

MURRAY (*staring down at her—with rough kindliness*). Here, here, that'll never do! You're not weeping about it, are you, silly? (*He pats her on the shoulder.*) What's the matter, Eileen? You didn't eat a thing this morning. I was watching you. (*With kindly severity.*) That's no way to gain weight, you know. You'll have to feed up. Do you hear what your guardian commands, eh?

EILEEN (*with dull hopelessness*). I know I'll lose again. I've been losing steadily the past three weeks.

MURRAY. Here! Don't you dare talk that way! I won't stand for it. Why, you've been picking up wonderfully—until just lately. You've made such a game fight for four months. Even the old Doc has told you how much he admired your pluck, and

69

how much better you were getting. You're not going to quit now, are you ?

EILEEN (*despairingly*). Oh, I don't care ! I don't care—now.

MURRAY. Now ? What do you mean by that ? What's happened to make things any different ?

EILEEN (*evasively*). Oh—nothing. Don't ask me, Stephen.

MURRAY (*with sudden anger*). I don't have to ask you. I can guess. Another letter from home—or from that ass, eh ?

EILEEN (*shaking her head*). No, it isn't that. (*She looks at him as if imploring him to comprehend.*)

MURRAY (*furiously*). Of course, you'd deny it. You always do. But don't you suppose I've got eyes ? It's been the same damn thing all the time you've been here. After every nagging letter—thank God they don't write often any more !—you've been all in ; and after their Sunday visits—you can thank God they've been few, too—you're utterly knocked out. It's a shame ! The selfish swine !

EILEEN. Stephen !

MURRAY (*relentlessly*). Don't be sentimental, Eileen. You know it's true. From what you've told me of their letters, their visits—from what I've seen and suspected—they've done nothing but worry and torment you and do their best to keep you from getting well.

EILEEN (*faintly*). You're not fair, Stephen.

70

MURRAY. Rot! When it isn't your father grumbling about expense, it's the kids, or that stupid housekeeper, or that slick Aleck, Nicholls, with his cowardly lies. Which is it this time?

EILEEN (*pitifully*). None of them.

MURRAY (*explosively*). But him, especially—the dirty cad! Oh, I've got a rich notion to pay a call on that gentleman when I leave and tell him what I think of him.

EILEEN (*quickly*). No—you mustn't ever! He's not to blame. If you knew—— (*She stops, lowering her eyes in confusion.*)

MURRAY (*roughly*). Knew what? You make me sick, Eileen—always finding excuses for him. I never could understand what a girl like you could see—— But what's the use? I've said all this before. You're wasting yourself on a—— (*Rudely.*) Love must be blind. And yet you say you don't love him, really?

EILEEN (*shaking her head—helplessly*). But I do—like Fred. We've been good friends so many years. I don't want to hurt him—his pride——

MURRAY. That's the same as answering no to my question. Then, if you don't love him, why don't you write and tell him to go to——break it off? (*Eileen bows her head, but doesn't reply. Irritated, Murray continues brutally.*) Are you afraid it would break his heart? Don't be a fool! The only way you could do that would be to deprive him of his meals.

EILEEN (*springing to her feet—distractedly*). Please

71

stop, Stephen! You're cruel! And you've been so kind—the only real friend I've had up here. Don't spoil it all now.

MURRAY (*remorsefully*). I'm sorry, Eileen. I was only talking. I won't say another word. (*Irritably.*) Still, someone ought to say or do something to put a stop to——

EILEEN (*with a broken laugh*). Never mind Everything will stop—soon, now!

MURRAY (*suspiciously*) What do you mean?

EILEEN (*with an attempt at a careless tone*). Nothing. If you can't see—— (*She turns to him with sudden intensity.*) Oh, Stephen, if you only knew how wrong you are about everything you've said. It's all true; but it isn't that—any of it—any more——that's—— Oh, I can't tell you!

MURRAY (*with great interest*). Please do, Eileen!

EILEEN (*with a helpless laugh*). No.

MURRAY. Please tell me what it is! Let me help you.

EILEEN. No. It wouldn't be any use, Stephen.

MURRAY (*offended*). Why do you say that? Haven't I helped before?

EILEEN. Yes—but this——

MURRAY. Come now! 'Fess up! What is "this"?

EILEEN. No. I couldn't speak of it here, anyway. They'll all be coming out soon

MURRAY (*insistently*). Then when? Where?

EILEEN. Oh, I don't know—perhaps never, no-where. I don't know—— Sometime before you leave, maybe.

MURRAY. But I may go to-morrow morning—if I gain weight and Stanton lets me.

EILEEN (*sadly*). Yes, I was forgetting—you were going right away. (*Dully.*) Then nowhere, I suppose —never. (*Glancing towards the dining-room.*) They're all getting up. Let's not talk about it any more—now.

MURRAY (*stubbornly*). But you'll tell me later, Eileen ? You must.

EILEEN (*vaguely*). Perhaps. It depends——

> (*The patients, about forty in number, straggle in from the dining-room by twos and threes, chatting in low tones. The men and women with few exceptions separate into two groups, the women congregating in the left right angle of chairs, the men sitting or standing in the right right angle. In appearance, most of the patients are tanned, healthy, and cheerful-looking. The great majority are under middle age. Their clothes are of the cheap, ready-made variety. They are all distinctly of the wage-earning class. They might well be a crowd of cosmopolitan factory workers gathered together after a summer vacation. A hollow-chestedness and a tendency to round shoulders may be detected as a common characteristic. A general air of tension, marked by frequent*

73

bursts of laughter in too high a key, seems to pervade the throng. Murray and Eileen, as if to avoid contact with the others, come over to the right in front of the dining-room door.)

MURRAY (*in a low voice*). Listen to them laugh. Did you ever notice—perhaps it's my imagination—how forced they act on Saturday mornings before they're weighed?

EILEEN (*dully*). No.

MURRAY. Can't you tell me that secret now? No one'll hear.

EILEEN (*vehemently*). No, no, how could I? Don't speak of it!

(A sudden silence falls on all the groups at once. Their eyes, by a common impulse, turn quickly towards the door to the hall.)

A WOMAN (*nervously—as if this moment's silent pause oppressed her.*) Play something, Peters. They ain't coming yet.

(Peters, a stupid-looking young fellow with a sly, twisted smirk which gives him the appearance of perpetually winking his eye, detaches himself from a group on the right. All join in with urging exclamations: " Go on, Peters! Go to it! Pedal up, Pete! Give us a rag! That's the boy, Peters!" etc.)

PETERS. Sure, if I got time.

*(He goes to the pianola and puts in a roll.
The mingled conversation and laughter
bursts forth again as he sits on the bench
and starts pedalling.)*

MURRAY *(disgustedly)*. It's sure good to think I
won't have to listen to that old tin-pan being banged
much longer !

*(The music interrupts him—a quick rag. The
patients brighten, hum, whistle, sway
their heads or tap their feet in time to the
tune. Doctor Stanton and Doctor Simms
appear in the doorway from the hall. All
eyes are turned on them.)*

STANTON *(raising his voice)*. They all seem to be
here, Doctor. We might as well start.

*(Mrs. Turner, the matron, comes in behind
them—a stout, motherly, capable-looking
woman with grey hair. She hears
Stanton's remark.)*

MRS. TURNER. And take temperatures after, Doctor ?

STANTON. Yes, Mrs. Turner. I think that's better
to-day.

MRS. TURNER. All right, Doctor.

*(Stanton and the assistant go out. Mrs.
Turner advances a step or so into the
room and looks from one group of patients
to the other, inclining her head and
smiling benevolently. All force smiles
and nod in recognition of her greeting.
Peters, at the pianolo, lets the music slow*

75

*down, glancing questioningly at the matron
to see if she is going to order it stopped.
Then, encouraged by her smile, his feet
pedal harder than ever.*)

MURRAY Look at old Mrs. Grundy's eyes pinned
on us! She'll accuse us of being too familiar again,
the old wench!

EILEEN. Ssshh. You're wrong. She's looking at
me, not at us.

MURRAY. At you? Why?

EILEEN. I ran a temperature yesterday. It must
have been over a hundred last night.

MURRAY (*with consoling scepticism*). You're always
looking for trouble, Eileen. How do you know you
ran a temp? You didn't see the stick, I suppose?

EILEEN. No—but—I could tell. I felt feverish and
chilly. It must have been way up.

MURRAY. Bosh! If it was you'd have been sent
to bed.

EILEEN. That's why she's looking at me. (*Pite-
ously.*) Oh, I do hope I won't be sent back to bed!
I don't know what I'd do. If I could only gain this
morning. If my temp has only gone down! (*Hopelessly.*) But I feel—— I didn't sleep a wink—
thinking——

MURRAY (*roughly*). You'll persuade yourself you've
got leprosy in a second. Don't be silly! It's all
imagination, I tell you. You'll gain. Wait and see
if you don't.

(*Eileen shakes her head. A metallic rumble*

76

and jangle comes from the hallway. Everyone turns in that direction with nervous expectancy.)

MRS. TURNER (*admonishingly*). Mr. Peters!

PETERS. Yes, ma'am.

(*He stops playing and rejoins the group of men on the right. In the midst of a silence broken only by hushed murmurs of conversation, Doctor Stanton appears in the hall doorway. He turns to help his assistant wheel in a Fairbanks scale on castors. They place the scale against the wall immediately to the rear of the doorway. Doctor Simms adjusts it to a perfect balance.*)

DOCTOR STANTON (*takes a pencil from his pocket and opens the record book he has in his hand*). All ready, Doctor?

DOCTOR SIMMS. Just a second, sir.

(*A chorus of coughs comes from the impatient crowd, and handkerchiefs are hurriedly produced to shield mouths.*)

MURRAY (*with a nervous smile*). Well, we're all set. Here's hoping!

EILEEN. You'll gain, I'm sure you will. You look so well.

MURRAY. Oh—I—I wasn't thinking of myself, I'm a sure thing. I was betting on you. I've simply got to gain to-day, when so much depends on it.

EILEEN. Yes, I hope you—— (*She falters brokenly and turns away from him.*)

DOCTOR SIMMS (*straightening up*). All ready, Doctor?

STANTON (*nods and glances at his book—without raising his voice—distinctly*). Mrs. Abner.

> (*A middle-aged woman comes and gets on the scale. Simms adjusts it to her weight of the previous week, which Stanton reads to him from the book in a low voice, and weighs her.*)

MURRAY (*with a relieved sigh*). They're off. (*Noticing Eileen's downcast head and air of dejection.*) Here! Buck up, Eileen! Old Lady Grundy's watching you —and it's your turn in a second.

> (*Eileen raises her head and forces a frightened smile. Mrs. Abner gets down off the scale with a pleased grin. She has evidently gained. She rejoins the group of women, chattering volubly in low tones. Her exultant " gained half a pound " can be heard. The other women smile their perfunctory congratulations, their eyes absent-minded, intent on their own worries. Stanton writes down the weight in the book.*)

STANTON. Miss Bailey. (*A young girl goes to the scales.*)

MURRAY. Bailey looks bad, doesn't she?

EILEEN (*her lips trembling*). She's been losing, too.

MURRAY. Well, *you're* going to gain to-day. Remember, now!

EILEEN (*with a feeble smile*).   I'll try to obey your orders.

> (*Miss Bailey goes down off the scales. Her eyes are full of despondency although she tries to make a brave face of it, forcing a laugh as she joins the women. They stare at her with pitying looks and murmur consoling phrases.*)

EILEEN.   She's lost again.   Oh, I wish I didn't have to get weighed——

STANTON.   Miss Carmody.

> (*Eileen starts nervously.*)

MURRAY (*as she leaves him*).   Remember now! Break the scales !

> (*She walks quickly to the scales, trying to assume an air of defiant indifference. The balance stays down as she steps up. Eileen's face shows her despair at this. Simms weighs her and gives the poundage in a low voice to Stanton. Eileen steps down mechanically, then hesitates as if not knowing where to turn, her anguished eyes flitting from one group to another.*)

MURRAY (*savagely*).   Damn !

> (*Doctor Stanton writes the figures in his book, glances sharply at Eileen, and then nods significantly to Mrs. Turner who is standing beside him.*)

STANTON (*calling the next*).   Miss Doeffler.

> (*Another woman comes to be weighed.*)

MRS. TURNER. Miss Carmody! Will **you** come here a moment, please?

EILEEN (*her face growing very pale*). Yes, Mrs. Turner.

(*The heads of the different groups bend together. Their eyes follow Eileen as they whisper. Mrs. Turner leads her down front, left. Behind them the weighing of the women continues briskly. The great majority have gained. Those who have not have either remained stationary or lost a negligible fraction of a pound. So, as the weighing proceeds, the general air of smiling satisfaction rises among the groups of women. Some of them, their ordeal over, go out through the hall doorway by twos and threes with suppressed laughter and chatter. As they pass behind Eileen they glance at her with pitying curiosity. Doctor Stanton's voice is heard at regular intervals calling the names in alphabetical order: Mrs. Elbing, Miss Finch, Miss Grimes, Miss Haines, Miss Hayes, Miss Jutner, Miss Linowski, Mrs. Marini, Mrs. McCoy, Miss McElroy, Miss Nelson, Mrs. Nott, Mrs. O'Brien, Mrs. Olson, Miss Paul, Miss Petrovski, Mrs. Quinn, Miss Robersi, Mrs. Stattler, Miss Unger.*)

MRS. TURNER (*putting her hand on Eileen's shoulder— kindly*). You're not looking so well lately, my dear, do you know it?

80

EILEEN (*bravely*). I feel—fine. (*Her eyes, as if looking for encouragement, seek Murray, who is staring at her worriedly.*)

MRS. TURNER (*gently*). You lost weight again, you know.

EILEEN. I know—but——

MRS. TURNER. This is the fourth week.

EILEEN. I—— I know it is——

MRS. TURNER. I've been keeping my eye on you. You seem—worried. Are you upset about—something we don't know?

EILEEN (*quickly*). No, no! I haven't slept much lately. That must be it.

MRS. TURNER. Are you worrying about your condition? Is that what keeps you awake?

EILEEN. No.

MRS. TURNER. You're sure it's not that?

EILEEN. Yes, I'm sure it's not, Mrs. Turner.

MRS. TURNER. I was going to tell you if you were: Don't do it! You can't expect it to be all smooth sailing. Even the most favourable cases have to expect these little setbacks. A few days' rest in bed will start you on the right trail again.

EILEEN (*in anguish, although she had realised this was coming*). Bed? Go back to bed? Oh, Mrs. Turner!

MRS. TURNER (*gently*). Yes, my dear, Doctor Stanton thinks it best. So when you go back to your cottage——

81

EILEEN.   Oh, please—not to-day—not right away !

MRS. TURNER.   You had a temperature and a high pulse yesterday, didn't you realise it ?   And this morning you look quite feverish. (*She tries to put her hand on Eileen's forehead, but the latter steps away defensively.*)

EILEEN.   It's only—not sleeping last night.   I was nervous.   Oh, I'm sure it'll go away.

MRS. TURNER (*consolingly*).   When you lie still and have perfect rest, of course it will.

EILEEN (*with a longing look over at Murray*).   But not to-day—please, Mrs. Turner.

MRS. TURNER (*looking at her keenly*).   There is something upsetting you.   You've something on your mind that you can't tell me, is that it ?   (*Eileen maintains a stubborn silence.*)   But think—*can't* you tell me ?   (*With a kindly smile.*)   I'm used to other people's troubles.   I've been playing mother-confessor to the patients for years now, and I think I've usually been able to help them.   Can't you confide in me, child ?   (*Eileen drops her eyes, but remains silent. Mrs. Turner glances mean'ngly over at Murray, who is watching them whenever he thinks the matron is not aware of it—a note of sharp rebuke in her voice.*)   I think I can guess your secret, my dear, even if you're too stubborn to tell.   This setback is your own fault.   You've let other notions become more important to you than the idea of getting well.   And you've no excuse for it.   After I had to warn you a month ago, I expected *that* silliness to stop instantly.

82

EILEEN (*her face flushed—protesting*). There never was anything. Nothing like that has anything to do with it.

MRS. TURNER (*sceptically*). What is it that has, then?

EILEEN (*lying determinedly*). It's my family. They keep writing—and worrying me—and—— That's what it is, Mrs. Turner.

MRS. TURNER (*not exactly knowing whether to believe this or not—probing the girl with her eyes*). Your father?

EILEEN. Yes, all of them. (*Suddenly seeing a way to discredit all of the matron's suspicions—excitedly.*) And principally the young man I'm engaged to—the one who came to visit me several times——

MRS. TURNER (*surprised*). So—you're engaged? (*Eileen nods. Mrs. Turner immediately dismisses her suspicions.*) Oh, pardon me. I didn't know that, you see, or I wouldn't—— (*She pats Eileen on the shoulder comfortingly.*) Never mind. You'll tell me all about it, won't you?

EILEEN (*desperately*). Yes. (*She seems about to go on, but the matron interrupts her.*)

MRS. TURNER. Oh, not here, my dear. Now now. Come to my room—let me see—I'll be busy all the morning—some time this afternoon. Will you do that?

EILEEN. Yes. (*Joyfully.*) Then I needn't go to bed right away?

MRS. TURNER. No—on one condition. You mustn't take any exercise. Stay in your recliner all day and rest and remain in bed to-morrow morning. And promise me you will rest and not worry any more about things we can easily fix up between us.

EILEEN. I promise, Mrs. Turner.

MRS. TURNER (*smiling in dismissal*). Very well, then. I must speak to Miss Bailey. I'll see you this afternoon.

EILEEN. Yes, Mrs. Turner.

> (*The matron goes to the rear where Miss Bailey is sitting with Mrs. Abner. She beckons to Miss Bailey, who gets up with a scared look, and they go to the far left corner of the room. Eileen stands for a moment hesitating—then starts to go to Murray, but just at this moment Peters comes forward and speaks to Murray.*)

PETERS (*with his sly twisted grin*). Say, Carmody musta lost fierce. Did yuh see the Old Woman handin' her an earful? Sent her back to bed, I betcha. What d'yuh think?

MURRAY (*impatiently, showing his dislike*). How the hell do I know?

PETERS (*sneeringly*). Huh, you don't know nothin' 'bout her, I s'pose? Where d'yuh get that stuff? Think yuh're kiddin' me?

MURRAY (*with cold rage before which the other slinks away*). Peters, the more I see of you the better I like a skunk! If it wasn't for other people losing

84

weight you couldn't get any joy out of life, could you? (*Roughly.*) Get away from me! (*He makes a threatening gesture.*)

PETERS (*beating a snarling retreat*). Wait'n' see if yuh don't lose too, yuh stuck-up boob!

> (*Seeing that Murray is alone again, Eileen starts towards him, but this time she is intercepted by Mrs. Abner, who stops on her way out. The weighing of the women is now finished, and that of the men, which proceeds much quicker, begins.*)

STANTON. Anderson!

> (*Anderson comes to the scales. The men all move down to the left to wait their turn, with the exception of Murray, who remains by the dining-room door, fidgeting impatiently, anxious for a word with Eileen.*)

MRS. ABNER (*taking Eileen's arm*). Coming over to the cottage, dearie?

EILEEN. Not just this minute, Mrs. Abner. I have to wait——

MRS. ABNER. For the Old Woman? You lost to-day, didn't you? Is she sendin' you to bed, the old devil?

EILEEN. Yes, I'm afraid I'll have to——

MRS. ABNER. She's a mean one, ain't she? I gained this week—half a pound. Lord, I'm gittin' fat! All my clothes are gittin' too small for me. Don't know what I'll do. Did you lose much, dearie?

85

EILEEN. Three pounds.

MRS. ABNER. Ain't that awful! (*Hastening to make up for this thoughtless remark.*) All the same, what's three pounds! You can git them back in a week after you're resting more. You been runnin' a temp, too, ain't you? (*Eileen nods.*) Don't worry about it, dearie. It'll go down. Worryin's the worst. Me, I don't never worry none. (*She chuckled with satisfaction—then soberly.*) I just been talkin' with Bailey. She's got to go to bed, too, I guess. She lost two pounds. She ain't runnin' no temp though.

STANTON. Barnes! (*Another man comes to the scales.*)

MRS. ABNER (*in a mysterious whisper*). Look at Mr. Murray, dearie. Ain't he nervous to-day? I don't know as I blame him, either. I heard the doctor said he'd let him go home if he gained to-day. Is it true, d'you know?

EILEEN (*dully*). I don't know.

MRS. ABNER. Gosh, I wish it was me! My old man's missin' me like the dickens, he writes. (*She starts to go.*) You'll be over to the cottage in a while, won't you? Me'n' you'll have a game of casino, eh?

EILEEN (*happy at this deliverance*). Yes, I'll be glad to.

STANTON. Cordero!

> (*Mrs. Abner goes out. Eileen again starts towards Murray, but this time Flynn, a young fellow with a brick-coloured, homely, good-natured face, and a shaven-necked*

*haircut, slouches back to Murray. Eileen
is brought to a halt in front of the table
where she stands, her face working with
nervous strain, clasping and unclasping
her trembling hands.)*

FLYNN *(curiously)*. Say, Steve, what's this bull
about the Doc lettin' yuh beat it if yuh gain to-day ?
Is it straight goods ?

MURRAY. He said he might, that's all. *(Impatiently.)* How the devil did that story get travelling
around ?

FLYNN *(with a grin)*. Wha' d'yuh expect with this
gang of skirts chewin' the fat ? Well, here's hopin'
yuh come home a winner, Steve.

MURRAY *(gratefully)*. Thanks. *(With confidence.)*
Oh, I'll gain all right ; but whether he'll let me go or
not—— *(He shrugs his shoulders.)*

FLYNN. Make 'em believe. I wish Stanton'd ask
waivers on me. *(With a laugh.)* I oughter gain a
ton to-day. I ate enough spuds for breakfast to
plant a farm.

STANTON. Flynn !

FLYNN. Me to the plate ! *(He strides to the scales.)*

MURRAY. Good luck !

> *(He starts to join Eileen, but Miss Bailey,
> who has finished her talk with Mrs.
> Turner, who goes out to the hall, approaches
> Eileen at just this moment. Murray stops
> in his tracks, fuming. He and Eileen
> exchange a glance of helpless annoyance.)*

MISS BAILEY (*her thin face full of the satisfaction of misery finding company—plucks at Eileen's sleeve*). Say, Carmody, she sent you back to bed, too, didn't she?

EILEEN (*absent-mindedly*). I suppose——

MISS BAILEY. You suppose? Don't you know? Of course she did. I got to go, too. (*Pulling Eileen's sleeve.*) Come on. Let's get out of here. I hate this place, don't you?

STANTON (*calling the next*). Hopper!

FLYNN (*shouts to Murray as he is going out to the hall*). I hit 'er for a two-bagger, Steve. Come on now, Bo, and bring me home! 'Atta, boy! (*Grinning gleefully, he slouches out. Doctor Stanton and all the patients laugh.*)

MISS BAILEY (*with irritating persistence*). Come on, Carmody. You've got to go to bed, too.

EILEEN (*at the end of her patience—releasing her arm from the other's grasp*). Let me alone, will you? I don't have to go to bed now—not till to-morrow morning.

MISS BAILEY (*despairingly, as if she couldn't believe her ears*). You don't have to go to bed?

EILEEN. Not now—no.

MISS BAILEY (*in a whining rage*). Why not? You've been running a temp, too, and I haven't. You must have a pull, that's what! It isn't fair. I'll bet you lost more than I did, too! What right have you got—— Well, I'm not going to bed if you don't. Wait 'n' see!

88

EILEEN (*turning away, revolted*). Go away! Leave me alone, please.

STANTON. Lowenstein!

MISS BAILEY (*turns to the hall door, whining*). All right for you! I'm going to find out. It isn't square. I'll write home.

> (*She disappears in the hallway. Murray strides over to Eileen, whose strength seems to have left her and who is leaning weakly against the table.*)

MURRAY. Thank God—at last! Isn't it hell—all these fools! I couldn't get to you. What did Old Lady Grundy have to say to you? I saw her giving me a hard look. Was it about us—the old stuff? (*Eileen nods with downcast eyes.*) What did she say? Never mind now. You can tell me in a minute. It's my turn next. (*His eyes glance towards the scales.*)

EILEEN (*intensely*). Oh, Stephen, I wish you weren't going away!

MURRAY (*excitedly*). Maybe I'm not. It's exciting —like gambling—if I win——

STANTON. Murray!

MURRAY. Wait here, Eileen.

> (*He goes to the scales. Eileen keeps her back turned. Her body stiffens rigidly in the intensity of her conflicting emotions. She stares straight ahead, her eyes full of anguish. Murray steps on the scales nervously. The balance rod hits the top smartly. He has gained. His face lights*

89

up and he heaves a great sigh of relief. Eileen seems to sense this outcome and her head sinks, her body sags weakly and seems to shrink to a smaller size. Murray gets off the scales, his face beaming with a triumphant smile. Doctor Stanton smiles and murmurs something to him in a low voice. Murray nods brightly; then turns back to Eileen.)

STANTON. Nathan! (*Another patient advances to the scales.*)

MURRAY (*trying to appear casual*). Well—three rousing cheers! Stanton told me to come to his office at eleven. That means a final exam—and release!

EILEEN (*dully*). So you gained?

MURRAY. Three pounds.

EILEEN. Funny—I lost three. (*With a pitiful effort at a smile*). I hope you gained the ones I lost. (*Her lips tremble.*) So you're surely going away.

MURRAY (*his joy fleeing as he is confronted with her sorrow—slowly*). It looks that way, Eileen.

EILEEN (*in a trembling whisper broken by rising sobs*). Oh—I'm so glad—you gained—the ones I lost, Stephen—— So glad! (*She breaks down, covering her face with her hands, stifling her sobs.*)

MURRAY (*alarmed*). Eileen! What's the matter? (*Desperately.*) Stop it! Stanton'll see you!

THE CURTAIN FALLS

Act Two: Scene Two

*Midnight of the same day. A cross-road near the
sanatorium. The main road comes down forward
from the right. A smaller road, leading down
from the left, joins it towards left centre.*

*Dense woods rise sheer from the grass and
bramble-grown ditches at the roadsides. At
the junction of the two roads there is a signpost,
its arms pointing towards the right and the left,
rear. A pile of round stones is at the road corner, left
forward. A full moon, riding high overhead, throws
the roads into white, shadowless relief and masses the
woods into walls of compact blackness. The trees
lean heavily together, their branches motionless,
unstirred by any trace of wind.*

*As the curtain rises, Eileen is discovered standing
in the middle of the road, front centre. Her face
shows white and clear in the bright moonlight as
she stares with anxious expectancy up the road to
the left. Her body is fixed in an attitude of rigid
immobility as if she were afraid the slightest movement would break the spell of silence and awaken
the unknown. She has shrunk instinctively as far
away as she can from the mysterious darkness*

*which rises at the roadsides like an imprisoning
wall. A sound of hurried footfalls, muffled by the
dust, comes from the road she is watching. She
gives a startled gasp. Her eyes strain to identify
the oncomer. Uncertain, trembling with fright,
she hesitates a second; then darts to the side of
the road and crouches down in the shadow.*

*Stephen Murray comes down the road from the
left. He stops by the signpost and peers about him.
He wears a cap, the peak of which casts his face into
shadow. Finally he calls in a low voice.*)

MURRAY. Eileen!

EILEEN (*coming out quickly from her hiding-place—
with a glad little cry*). Stephen! At last! (*She
runs to him as if she were going to fling her arms about
him, but stops abashed. He reaches out and takes her
hands.*)

MURRAY. At last? It can't be twelve yet. (*He
leads her to the pile of stones on the left.*) I haven't
heard the village clock.

EILEEN. I must have come early. It seemed as if
I'd been waiting for ages. I was so anxious——

MURRAY. How your hands tremble! Were you
frightened?

EILEEN (*forcing a smile*). A little. The woods
are so black—and queer-looking. I'm all right now.

MURRAY. Sit down. You must rest. (*In a tone of
annoyed reproof.*) I'm going to read you a lecture,
young lady. You shouldn't ever have done this—
running a temp and—— Good heavens, don't you
want to get well?

EILEEN (*dully*). I don't know——

MURRAY (*irritably*). You make me ill when you talk that way, Eileen. It doesn't sound like you at all. What's come over you lately? Get a grip on yourself, for God's sake. I was—knocked out— when I read the note you slipped me after supper. I didn't get a chance to read it until late, I was so busy packing, and by that time you'd gone to your cottage. If I could have reached you any way I'd have refused to come here, I tell you straight. But I couldn't—and I knew you'd be here waiting—and —still, I feel guilty. Damn it, this isn't the thing for you! You ought to be in bed asleep. Can't you look out for yourself?

EILEEN (*humbly*). Please, Stephen, don't scold me.

MURRAY. How the devil did you ever get the idea —meeting me here at this ungodly hour?

EILEEN. You'd told me about your sneaking out that night to go to the village, and I thought there'd be no harm this one night—the last night.

MURRAY. But I'm well. I've been well. It's different. You—— Honest, Eileen, you shouldn't lose sleep and tax your strength.

EILEEN. Don't scold me, please. I'll make up for it. I'll rest all the time—after you're gone. I just had to see you some way—somewhere where there weren't eyes and ears on all sides—when you told me after dinner that Doctor Stanton had examined you and said you could go to-morrow—— (*A clock in the distant village begins striking.*) Ssshh! Listen.

MURRAY. That's twelve now. You see I was early.

(*In a pause of silence they wait motionlessly until the last mournful note dies in the hushed woods.*)

EILEEN (*in a stifled voice*). It isn't to-morrow now, is it? It's to-day—the day you're going.

MURRAY (*something in her voice making him avert his face and kick at the heap of stones on which she is sitting—brusquely*). Well, I hope you took precautions so you wouldn't be caught sneaking out.

EILEEN. I did just what you'd told me you did—stuffed the pillows under the clothes so the watchman would think I was there.

MURRAY. None of the patients on your porch saw you leave, did they?

EILEEN. No. They were all asleep.

MURRAY. That's all right, then. I wouldn't trust any of that bunch of women. They'd be only too glad to squeal on you. (*There is an uncomfortable pause. Murray seems waiting for her to speak. He looks about him at the trees, up into the moonlit sky, breathing in the fresh air with a healthy delight. Eileen remains with downcast head, staring at the road.*) It's beautiful to-night, isn't it? Worth losing sleep for.

EILEEN (*dully*). Yes. (*Another pause—finally she murmurs faintly.*) Are you leaving early?

MURRAY. The ten-forty. Leave the San at ten, I guess.

EILEEN. You're going home?

MURRAY. Home ? You mean to the town ? No. But I'm going to see my sisters—just to say hello. I've got to, I suppose. I won't stay more than a few days, if I can help it.

EILEEN. I'm sure—I've often felt—you're unjust to your sisters. (*With conviction.*) I'm sure they must both love you.

MURRAY (*frowning*). Maybe, in their own way. But what's love without a glimmer of understanding —a nuisance ! They have never seen the real me and never have wanted to—that's all.

EILEEN (*as if to herself*). What is—the real you ? (*Murray kicks at the stones impatiently without answering. Eileen hastens to change the subject.*) And then you'll go to New York ?

MURRAY (*interested at once*). Yes. You bet.

EILEEN. And write more ?

MURRAY. Not in New York, no. I'm going there to take a vacation, and live, really enjoy myself for a while. I've enough money for that as it is, and if the other stories you typed sell—I'll be as rich as Rockefeller. I might even travel—— No, I've got to make good with my best stuff first. I'll save the travelling as a reward, a prize to gain. That'll keep me at it. I know what I'll do. When I've had enough of New York, I'll rent a place in the country —some old farmhouse—and live alone there and work. (*Lost in his own plans—with pleasure.*) That's the right idea, isn't it ?

EILEEN (*trying to appear enthused*). It ought to

be fine for your work. (*After a pause.*) They're fine, those stories you wrote here. They're—so much like you. I'd know it was you wrote them even if— I didn't know.

MURRAY (*pleased*). Wait till you read the others I'm going to do! (*After a slight pause—with a good-natured grin*). Here I am talking about myself again! Why don't you call me down when I start that drivel? But you don't know how good it is to have your dreams coming true. It'd make an egotist out of anyone.

EILEEN (*sadly*). No. I don't know. But I love to hear you talk of yours.

MURRAY (*with an embarrassed laugh*). Thanks. Well, I've certainly told you all of them. You're the only one—— (*He stops and abruptly changes the subject.*) You said in your note that you had something important to tell me. (*He sits down beside her, crossing his legs.*) Is it about your interview with Old Mrs. Grundy this afternoon?

EILEEN. No, that didn't amount to anything. She seemed mad because I told her so little. I think she guessed I only told her what I did so she'd let me stay up, maybe—your last day,—and to keep her from thinking what she did—about us.

MURRAY (*quickly, as if he wishes to avoid this subject*). What is it you wanted to tell me, then?

EILEEN (*sadly*). It doesn't seem so important now, somehow. I suppose it was silly of me to drag you out here, just for that. It can't mean anything to you—much.

MURRAY (*encouragingly*). How do you know it can't?

EILEEN (*slowly*). I only thought—you might like to know.

MURRAY (*interestedly*). Know what? What is it? If I can help——

EILEEN. No. (*After a moment's hesitation.*) I wrote to him this afternoon.

MURRAY. Him?

EILEEN. The letter you've been advising me to write.

MURRAY (*as if the knowledge of this alarmed him—haltingly*). You mean—Fred Nicholls?

EILEEN. Yes.

MURRAY (*after a pause—uncomfortably*). You mean —you broke it all off?

EILEEN. Yes—for good. (*She looks up at his averted face. He remains silent. She continues apprehensively.*) You don't say anything. I thought—you'd be glad. You've always told me it was the honourable thing to do.

MURRAY (*gruffly*). I know. I say more than my prayers, damn it! (*With sudden eagerness.*) Have you mailed the letter yet?

EILEEN. Yes. Why?

MURRAY (*shortly*). Humph. Oh—nothing.

EILEEN (*with pained disappointment*). Oh, Stephen, you don't think I did wrong, do you—now—after all you've said?

MURRAY (*hurriedly*). Wrong? No, not if you were convinced it was the right thing to do yourself —if you know you don't love him. But I'd hate to think you did it just on my advice. I shouldn't—— I didn't mean to interfere. I don't know enough about your relations for my opinion to count.

EILEEN (*hurt*). You know all there is to know.

MURRAY. I didn't mean—anything like that. I know you've been frank. But him—I don't know him. How could I, just meeting him once? He may be quite different from my idea. That's what I'm getting at. I don't want to be unfair to him.

EILEEN (*bitterly scornful*). You needn't worry. You weren't unfair. And you needn't be afraid you were responsible for my writing. I'd been going to for a long time before you ever spoke.

MURRAY (*with a relieved sigh*). I'm glad of that— honestly, Eileen. I felt guilty. I shouldn't have knocked him behind his back without knowing him at all.

EILEEN. You said you could read him like a book from his letters I showed you.

MURRAY (*apologetically*). I know. I'm a fool.

EILEEN (*angrily*). What makes you so considerate of Fred Nicholls all of a sudden? What you thought about him was right.

MURRAY (*vaguely*). I don't know. One makes mistakes.

EILEEN (*assertively*). Well, I know! You needn't waste pity on him. He'll be only too glad to get my letter. He's been anxious to be free of me ever since I was sent here, only he thought it wouldn't be decent to break it off himself while I was sick. He was afraid of what people would say about him when they found it out. So he's just gradually stopped writing and coming for visits, and waited for me to realise. And if I didn't, I know he'd have broken it off himself the first day I got home. I've kept persuading myself that, in spite of the way he's acted, he did love me as much as he could love anyone, and that it would hurt him if I—— But now I know that he never loved me, that he couldn't love anyone but himself. Oh, I don't hate him for it. He can't help being what he is. And all people seem to be—like that, mostly. I'm only going to remember that he and I grew up together, and that he was kind to me then when he thought he liked me—and forget all the rest. (*With agitated impatience.*) Oh, Stephen, you know all this I've said about him. Why don't you admit it? You've read his letters.

MURRAY (*haltingly*). Yes, I'll admit that was my opinion—only I wanted to be sure you'd found out for yourself.

EILEEN (*defiantly*). Well, I have! You see that now, don't you?

MURRAY. Yes; and I'm glad you're free of him, for your own sake. I knew he wasn't the person. (*With an attempt at a joking tone.*) You must get one of the right sort—next time.

EILEEN (*springing to her feet with a cry of pain*). Stephen!

99

(He avoids her eyes, which search his face pleadingly.)

MURRAY *(mumbling)*. He wasn't good enough—to lace your shoes—nor anyone else, either.

EILEEN *(with a nervous laugh)*. Don't be silly. *(After a pause, during which she waits hungrily for some word from him—with a sigh of despair—faintly.)* Well, I've told you—all there is. I might as well go back.

MURRAY *(not looking at her—indistinctly)*. Yes. You mustn't lose too much sleep. I'll come to your cottage in the morning to say good-bye. They'll permit that, I guess.

EILEEN *(stands looking at him imploringly, her face convulsed with anguish, but he keeps his eyes fixed on the rocks at his feet. Finally she seems to give up and takes a few uncertain steps up the road towards the right —in an exhausted whisper)*. Good night, Stephen.

MURRAY *(his voice choked and husky)*. Good night, Eileen.

EILEEN *(walks weakly up the road, but, as she passes the signpost, she suddenly stops and turns to look again at Murray, who has not moved or lifted his eyes. A great shuddering sob shatters her pent-up emotions. She runs back to Murray, her arms outstretched, with a choking cry)*. Stephen!

MURRAY *(startled, whirls to face her and finds her arms thrown around his neck—in a terrified tone)*. Eileen!

EILEEN (*brokenly*). I love you, Stephen—you! That's what I wanted to tell!

> (*She gazes up into his eyes, her face trans-figured by the joy and pain of this abject confession.*)

MURRAY (*wincing as if this were the thing he had feared to hear*). Eileen!

EILEEN (*pulling down his head with fierce strength and kissing him passionately on the lips*). I love you! I will say it! There! (*With sudden horror.*) Oh, I know I shouldn't kiss you! I mustn't! You're all well—and I——

MURRAY (*protesting frenziedly*). Eileen! Damn it! Don't say that! What do you think I am!

> (*He kisses her fiercely two or three times until she forces a hand over her mouth.*)

EILEEN (*with a hysterically happy laugh*). No! Just hold me in your arms—just a little while—before——

MURRAY (*his voice trembling*). Eileen! Don't talk that way! You're—it's killing me. I can't stand it!

EILEEN (*with soothing tenderness*). Listen, dear—listen—and you won't say a word—I've so much to say—till I get through—please, will you promise?

MURRAY (*between clinched teeth*). Yes—anything, Eileen!

EILEEN. Then I want to say—I know your secret. You don't love me—Isn't that it? (*Murray groans.*) Ssshh! It's all right, dear. You can't help what you don't feel. I've guessed you didn't—right along. And I've loved you—such a long time now—always, it seems. And you've sort of guessed—that I did—didn't you ? No, don't speak ! I'm sure you've guessed—only you didn't want to know—that—did you ?—when you didn't love me. That's why you were lying—but I saw, I knew ! Oh, I'm not blaming you, darling. How could I—never ! You mustn't look so—so frightened. I know how you felt, dear. I've—I've watched you. It was just a flirtation for you at first. Wasn't it ? Oh, I know. It was just fun, and—— Please don't look at me so. I'm not hurting you, am I ? I wouldn't for worlds, dear—you know—hurt you ! And then afterwards—you found we could be such good friends—helping each other—and you wanted it to stay just like that always, didn't you ?—I know—and then I had to spoil it all —and fall in love with you—didn't I ? Oh, it was stupid—I shouldn't—I couldn't help it, you were so kind and—and different—and I wanted to share in your work and—and everything. I knew you wouldn't want to know I loved you—when you didn't —and I tried hard to be fair and hide my love so you wouldn't see—and I did, didn't I, dear ? You never knew till just lately—maybe not till just to-day—did you ?—when I knew you were going away so soon—and couldn't help showing it. You never knew before, did you ? Did you ?

MURRAY (*miserably*). No. Oh, Eileen—Eileen, I'm so sorry !

EILEEN (*in heart-broken protest*). Sorry ? Oh, no,.

Stephen, you mustn't be! It's been beautiful—all of it—for me! That's what makes your going—so hard. I had to see you to-night—I'd have gone—crazy—if I didn't know you knew, if I hadn't made you guess. And I thought—if you knew about my writing to Fred—that—maybe—it'd make some difference. (*Murray groans—and she laughs hysterically.*) I must have been crazy—to think that—mustn't I? As if that could—when you don't love me. Sshh! Please! Let me finish. You mustn't feel sad—or anything. It's made me happier than I've ever been—loving you—even when I did know—you didn't. Only now—you'll forgive me telling you all this, won't you, dear? Now, it's so terrible to think I won't see you any more. I'll feel so—without anybody.

MURRAY (*brokenly*). But I'll—come back. And you'll be out soon—and then——

EILEEN (*brokenly*). Sshh! Let me finish. You don't know how alone I am now. Father—he'll marry that housekeeper—and the children—they've forgotten me. None of them need me any more. They've found out how to get on without me—and I'm a drag—dead to them—no place for me home any more—and they'll be afraid to have me back—afraid of catching—I know she won't want me back. And Fred—he's gone—he never mattered, anyway. Forgive me, dear—worrying you—only I want you to know how much you've meant to me—so you won't forget—ever—after you've gone.

MURRAY (*in grief-stricken tones*). Forget? Eileen! I'll do anything in God's world——

103

EILEEN. I know—you like me a lot even if you can't love me—don't you? (*His arms tighten about her as he bends down and forces a kiss on her lips again.*) Oh, Stephen! That was for good-bye. You mustn't come to-morrow morning. I couldn't bear having you—with people watching. But you'll write after —often—won't you? (*Heart-brokenly.*) Oh, please do that, Stephen!

MURRAY. I will! I swear! And when you get out I'll—we'll—I'll find something. (*He kisses her again.*)

EILEEN (*breaking away from him with a quick movement and stepping back a few feet*). Good-bye, darling. Remember me—and perhaps—you'll find out after a time—I'll pray God to make it so! Oh, what am I saying? Only—I'll hope—I'll hope—till I die!

MURRAY (*in anguish*). Eileen!

EILEEN (*her breath coming in tremulous heaves of her bosom*). Remember, Stephen—if ever you want —I'll do anything—anything you want—no matter what—I don't care—there's just you and—don't hate me, dear. I love you—love you—remember! (*She suddenly turns and runs away up the road.*)

MURRAY. Eileen! (*He starts to run after her, but stops by the signpost and stamps on the ground furiously, his fists clenched in impotent rage at himself and at fate. He curses hoarsely.*) Christ!

THE CURTAIN FALLS

The Straw
Act Three

Act Three

Four months later. An isolation room at the Infirmary with a sleeping porch at the right of it. Late afternoon of a Sunday towards the end of October. The room, extending two-thirds of the distance from left to right, is, for reasons of space economy, scantily furnished with the bare necessities—a bureau with mirror in the left corner, rear—two straight-backed chairs—a table with a glass top in the centre. The floor is varnished hardwood. The walls and furniture are painted white. On the left, forward, a door to the hall. On the right, rear, a double glass door opening on the porch. Farther front two windows. The porch, a screened-in continuation of the room, contains only a single iron bed, painted white, and a small table placed beside the bed.

The woods, the leaves of the trees rich in their autumn colouring, rise close about this side of the Infirmary. Their branches almost touch the porch on the right. In the rear of the porch they have been cleared away from the building for a narrow space, and through this opening the distant hills can be seen with the tree tops glowing in the sunlight.

*As the curtain rises, Eileen is discovered lying
in the bed on the porch, propped up into a half-
sitting position by pillows under her back and head.
She seems to have grown much thinner. Her
face is pale and drawn, with deep hollows under
her cheek-bones. Her eyes are dull and lustreless.
She gazes straight before her into the wood with
the unseeing stare of apathetic indifference. The
door from the hall in the room behind her is opened,
and Miss Howard enters, followed by Bill Carmody,
Mrs. Brennan, and Mary. Carmody's manner is
unwontedly sober and subdued. This air of respect-
able sobriety is further enhanced by a black suit,
glaringly new and stiffly pressed, a new black
derby hat, and shoes polished like a mirror. His
expression is full of a bitter, if suppressed, resentment. His gentility is evidently forced upon him
in spite of himself and correspondingly irksome.
Mrs. Brennan is a tall, stout woman of fifty, lusty
and loud-voiced, with a broad, snub-nosed, florid
face, a large mouth, the upper lip darkened by a
suggestion of moustache, and little round blue eyes,
hard and restless with a continual fuming irritation.
She is got up regardless in her ridiculous Sunday-
best. Mary appears tall and skinny-legged in a
starched, outgrown frock. The sweetness of her face
has disappeared, giving way to a hang-dog sullen-
ness, a stubborn silence, with sulky, furtive glances
of rebellion directed at her step-mother.*

MISS HOWARD (*pointing to the porch*). She's out
there on the porch.

MRS. BRENNAN (*with dignity*).   Thank you, ma'am.

MISS HOWARD (*with a searching glance at the visitors as if to appraise their intentions*).   Eileen's been very sick lately, you know, so be careful not to worry her about anything.   Do your best to cheer her up.

CARMODY (*mournfully*).   We'll try to put life in her spirits, God help her. (*With an uncertain look at Mrs. Brennan.*)   Won't we, Maggie?

MRS. BRENNAN (*turning sharply on Mary, who has gone over to examine the things on the bureau*).   Come away from that, Mary.   Curiosity killed a cat.   Don't be touchin' her things.   Remember what I told you. Or is it admirin' your mug in the mirror you are? (*Turning to Miss Howard as Mary moves away from the bureau, hanging her head—shortly.*)   Don't you worry, ma'am.   We won't trouble Eileen at all.

MISS HOWARD.   Another thing.   You mustn't say anything to her of what Miss Gilpin just told you about her being sent away to the State Farm in a few days.   Eileen isn't to know till the very last minute.   It would only disturb her.

CARMODY (*hastily*).   We'll not say a word of it.

MISS HOWARD (*turning to the hall door*).   Thank you.

(*She goes out, shutting the door.*)

MRS. BRENNAN (*angrily*).   She has a lot of impudent gab, that one, with her don't do this and don't do that!   It's a wonder you wouldn't speak up to her and shut her mouth, you great fool, and you payin' money to give her her job. (*Disgustedly.*)   You've no guts in you.

CARMODY (*placatingly*). Would you have me raisin'
a shindy when Eileen's leavin' here in a day or more ?
What'd be the use ?

MRS. BRENNAN. In the new place she's goin' you'll
not have to pay a cent, and that's a blessing ! It's
small good they've done her here for all the money
they've taken. (*Gazing about the room critically.*)
It's neat and clean enough ; and why shouldn't it,
a tiny room and the lot of them nothing to do all
day but scrub. (*Scornfully.*) Two sticks of chairs
and a table ! They don't give much for the money.

CARMODY. Catch them ! It's a good thing she's
clearin' out of this, and her worse off after them
curin' her eight months than she was when she came.
She'll maybe get well in the new place.

MRS. BRENNAN (*indifferently*). It's God's will,
what'll happen. (*Irritably.*) And I'm thinkin' it's
His punishment she's under now for having no heart
in her and never writin' home a word to you or the
children in two months or more. If the doctor
hadn't wrote us himself to come see her, she was
sick, we'd have been no wiser.

CARMODY. Whisht ! Don't be blamin' a sick girl.

MARY (*who has drifted to one of the windows at
right—curiously*). There's somebody in bed out
there. I can't see her face. Is it Eileen ?

MRS. BRENNAN. Don't be goin' out there till I
tell you, you imp ! I must speak to your father first.
(*Coming closer to him and lowering her voice.*) Are
you going to tell her about it ?

CARMODY (*pretending ignorance*). About what?

MRS. BRENNAN. About what, indeed! Don't pretend you don't know. About our marryin' two weeks back, of course. What else?

CARMODY (*uncertainly*). Yes—I disremembered she didn't know. I'll have to tell her, surely.

MRS. BRENNAN (*flaring up*). You speak like you wouldn't. Is it shamed of me you are? Are you afraid of a slip of a girl? Well, then, I'm not! I'll tell her to her face soon enough.

CARMODY (*angry in his turn—assertively*). You'll not, now! Keep your mouth out of this and your rough tongue! I tell you I'll tell her.

MRS. BRENNAN (*satisfied*). Let's be going out to her, then. (*They move towards the door to the porch.*) And keep your eye on your watch. We mustn't miss the train. Come with us, Mary, and remember to keep your mouth shut.

> (*They go out on the porch and stand just outside the door waiting for Eileen to notice them; but the girl in bed continues to stare into the woods, oblivious to their presence.*)

MRS. BRENNAN (*nudging Carmody with her elbow—in a harsh whisper*). She don't see us. It's a dream she's in with her eyes open. Glory be, it's bad she's lookin'. The look on her face'd frighten you. Speak to her, you!

> (*Eileen stirs uneasily as if this whisper had disturbed her unconsciously.*)

CARMODY (*wetting his lips and clearing his throat huskily*). Eileen.

EILEEN (*startled, turns and stares at them with frightened eyes. After a pause she ventures uncertainly, as if she were not sure but what these figures might be creatures of her dream*). Father. (*Her eyes shift to Mrs. Brennan's face and she shudders.*) Mrs. Brennan.

MRS. BRENNAN (*quickly—in a voice meant to be kindly*). Here we are, all of us, come to see you. How is it you're feelin' now, Eileen?

> (*While she is talking she advances to the bedside, followed by Carmody, and takes one of the sick girl's hands in hers. Eileen withdraws it as if stung and holds it out to her father. Mrs. Brennan's face flushes angrily and she draws back from the bedside.*)

CARMODY (*moved—with rough tenderness patting her hand*). Ah, Eileen, sure it's a sight for sore eyes to see you again! (*He bends down as if to kiss her, but, struck by a sudden fear, hesitates, straightens himself, and shamed by the understanding in Eileen's eyes, grows red and stammers confusedly.*) How are you now? Sure it's the picture of health you're lookin'.

> (*Eileen sighs and turns her eyes away from him with a resigned sadness.*)

MRS. BRENNAN. What are you standin' there for like a stick, Mary? Haven't you a word to say to your sister?

EILEEN (*twisting her head around and seeing Mary*

for the first time—with a glad cry.) Mary! I—why, I didn't see you before! Come here.

> (*Mary approaches gingerly with apprehensive side glances at Mrs. Brennan, who watches her grimly. Eileen's arms reach out for her hungrily. She grasps her about the waist and seems trying to press the unwilling child to her breast.*)

MARY (*fidgeting nervously—suddenly in a frightened whine.*) Let me go! (*Eileen releases her, looks at her face dazedly for a second, then falls back limply with a little moan and shuts her eyes. Mary, who has stepped back a pace, remains fixed there as if fascinated with fright by her sister's face. She stammers.*) Eileen—you look so—so funny.

EILEEN (*without opening her eyes—in a dead voice*). You, too! I never thought you—— Go away, please.

MRS. BRENNAN (*with satisfaction*). Come here to me, Mary, and don't be botherin' your sister.

> (*Mary avoids her step-mother, but retreats to the far end of the porch where she stands shrunk back against the wall, her eyes fixed on Eileen with the same fascinated horror.*)

CARMODY (*after an uncomfortable pause, forcing himself to speak*). Is the pain bad, Eileen?

EILEEN (*dully—without opening her eyes*). There's no pain. (*There is another pause—then she murmurs indifferently*). There are chairs in the room you can bring out if you want to sit down.

113

MRS. BRENNAN (*sharply*). We've not time to be sittin'. We've the train back to catch.

EILEEN (*in the same lifeless voice*). It's a disagreeable trip. I'm sorry you had to come.

CARMODY (*fighting against an oppression he cannot understand, bursts into a flood of words*). Don't be talking of the trip. Sure we're glad to take it to get a sight of you. It's three months since I've had a look at you, and I was anxious. Why haven't you written a line to us? You could do that without trouble, surely. Don't you ever think of us at all any more? (*He waits for an answer, but Eileen remains silent with her eyes closed. Carmody starts to walk up and down, talking with an air of desperation.*) You're not asking a bit of news from home. I'm thinkin' the people out here have taken all the thought of us out of your head. We're all well, thank God. I've another good job on the streets from Murphy and one that'll last a long time, praise be! I'm needin' it surely, with all the expenses—but no matter. Billy had a raise from his old skinflint of a boss a month back. He's gettin' seven a week now and proud as a turkey. He was comin' out with us to-day, but he'd a date with his girl. Sure, he's got a girl now, the young bucko! What d'you think of him? It's old Malloy's girl he's after—the pop-eyed one with glasses, you remember—as ugly as a blind sheep, only he don't think so. He said to give you his love. (*Eileen stirs and sighs wearily, a frown appearing for an instant on her forehead.*) And Tom and Nora was comin' out too, but Father Fitz had some doin's or

114

other up to the school, and he told them to be there, so they wouldn't come with us, but they sent their love to you, too. They're growin' so big you'd not know them. Tom's no good at the school. He's like Billy was. I've had to take the strap to him often. He's always playin' hooky and roamin' the streets. And Nora. (*With pride.*) There's the divil for you! Up to everything she is and no holdin' her high spirits. As pretty as a picture, and the smartest girl in her school, Father Fitz says. Am I lyin', Maggie?

MRS. BRENNAN (*grudgingly*). She's smart enough—and too free with her smartness.

CARMODY (*pleased*). Ah, don't be talkin'! She'll know more than the lot of us before she's grown even. (*He pauses in his walk and stares down at Eileen, frowning.*) Are you sick, Eileen, that you're keepin' your eyes shut without a word out of you?

EILEEN (*wearily*). No. I'm tired, that's all.

CARMODY (*resuming his walk*). And who else is there, let me think? Oh, Mary—she's the same as ever, you can see for yourself.

EILEEN (*bitterly*). The same? Oh, no!

CARMODY. She's grown, you mean? I suppose. You'd notice, not seeing her so long?

> (*He can think of nothing else to say, but walks up and down with a restless, uneasy expression.*)

MRS. BRENNAN (*sharply*). What time is it gettin'?

CARMODY (*fumbles for his watch*). Half-past four, a bit after.

MRS. BRENNAN. We'll have to leave soon. It's a long jaunt down that hill in that buggy.

> (*She catches his eye and makes violent signs to him to tell Eileen what he has come to tell.*)

CARMODY (*after an uncertain pause—clenching his fists and clearing his throat*). Eileen.

EILEEN. Yes.

CARMODY (*irritably*). Can't you open your eyes on me? It's like talkin' to myself I am.

EILEEN (*looking at him—dully*). What is it?

CARMODY (*stammering—avoiding her glance*). It's this, Eileen—me and Maggie—Mrs. Brennan, that is—we——

EILEEN (*without surprise*). You're going to marry her?

CARMODY (*with an effort*). Not goin' to. It's done.

EILEEN (*without a trace of feeling*). Oh, so you've been married already?

> (*Without further comment, she closes her eyes.*)

CARMODY. Two weeks back we were, by Father Fitz.

> (*He stands staring down at his daughter, irritated, perplexed and confounded by her silence, looking as if he longed to shake her.*)

116

MRS. BRENNAN (*angry at the lack of enthusiasm shown by Eileen*). Let us get out of this, Bill. We're not wanted, that's plain as the nose on your face. It's little she's caring about you, and little thanks she has for all you've done for her and the money you've spent.

CARMODY (*with a note of pleading*). Is that a proper way to be treatin' your father, Eileen, after what I've told you? Have you no heart in you at all? Is it nothin' to you you've a good, kind woman now for mother?

EILEEN (*fiercely, her eyes flashing open on him*). No, no! Never!

MRS. BRENNAN (*plucking at Carmody's elbow. He stands looking at Eileen helplessly, his mouth open, a guilty flush spreading over his face*). Come out of here, you big fool, you! Is it to listen to insults to your livin' wife you're waiting? Am I to be tormented and you never raise a hand to stop her?

CARMODY (*turning on her threateningly*). Will you shut your gab?

EILEEN (*with a moan*). Oh, go away, Father! Please! Take her away!

MRS. BRENNAN (*pulling at his arm*). Take me away this second or I'll go on without you and never speak again to you till the day I die!

CARMODY (*pushes her violently away from him—raging, his fist uplifted*). Shut your gab, I'm saying!

MRS. BRENNAN. The divil mend you and yours then! I'm leavin' you. (*She starts for the door.*)

CARMODY (*hastily*). Wait a bit, Maggie. I'm comin'. (*She goes into the room, slamming the door, but once inside she stands still, trying to listen. Carmody glares down at his daughter's pale twitching face with the closed eyes. Finally he croaks in a whining tone of fear.*) Is your last word a cruel one to me this day, Eileen?

> (*She remains silent. His face darkens. He turns and strides out of the door. Mary darts after him with a frightened cry of " Papa." Eileen covers her face with her hands and a shudder of relief runs over her body.*)

MRS. BRENNAN (*as Carmody enters the room—in a mollified tone*). So you've come, have you? Let's go, then? (*Carmody stands looking at her in silence, his expression full of gloomy rage. She bursts out impatiently.*) Are you comin' or are you goin' back to her? (*She grabs Mary's arm and pushes her towards the door to the hall.*) Are you comin' or not, I'm askin'?

CARMODY (*sombrely—as if to himself*). There's something wrong in the whole of this—that I can't make out. (*With sudden fury he brandishes his fists as though defying someone and growls threateningly.*) And I'll get drunk this night—dead, rotten drunk! (*He seems to detect disapproval in Mrs. Brennan's face, for he shakes his fist at her and repeats like a solemn oath.*) I'll get drunk this night, I'm sayin'! I'll get drunk if my soul roasts for it—and no one in the whole world is strong enough to stop me!

118

(*Mrs. Brennan turns from him with a dis-*
gusted shrug of her shoulders and hustles
Mary out of the door. Carmody, after a
second's pause, follows them. Eileen lies
still, looking out into the woods with empty,
desolate eyes. Miss Howard comes into
the room from the hall and goes to the
porch, carrying a glass of milk in her
hand.)

MISS HOWARD. Here's your diet, Eileen. I forgot
it until just now. Sundays are awful days, aren't
they? They get me all mixed up in my work, with
all these visitors around. Did you have a nice visit
with your folks?

EILEEN (*forcing a smile*). Yes.

MISS HOWARD. You look worn out. I hope they
didn't worry you over home affairs?

EILEEN. No.

(*She sips her milk and sets it back on the table*
with a shudder of disgust.)

MISS HOWARD (*with a smile*). What a face! You'd
think you were taking poison.

EILEEN. I hate it! (*With deep passion.*) I wish
it was poison!

MISS HOWARD (*jokingly*). Oh, come now! That
isn't a nice way to feel on the Sabbath. (*With a*
meaning smile.) I've some news that'll cheer you up,
I bet. (*Archly.*) Guess who's here on a visit?

EILEEN (*startled—in a frightened whisper*). Who?

119

MISS HOWARD. Mr. Murray. (*Eileen closes her eyes wincingly for a moment and a shadow of pain comes over her face.*) He just came about the time your folks did. I saw him for a moment, not to speak to. He was going to the main building—to see Doctor Stanton, I suppose. (*Beaming—with a certain curiosity.*) What do you think of that for news?

EILEEN (*trying to conceal her agitation and assume a casual tone*). He must have come to be examined.

MISS HOWARD (*with a meaning laugh*). Oh, I'd hardly say that was his main reason. He does look much thinner and very tired, though. I suppose he's been working too hard. (*In business-like tones.*) Well, I've got to get back on the job. (*She turns to the door calling back jokingly.*) He'll be in to see you, of course, so look your prettiest.

> (*She goes out and shuts the door to the porch. Eileen gives a frightened gasp and struggles up in bed as if she wanted to call the nurse to return. Then she lies back in a state of great nervous excitement, twisting her head with eager, fearful glances towards the door, listening, clasping and unclasping her thin fingers on the white spread. As Miss Howard walks across the room to the hall door, it is opened and Stephen Murray enters. A great change is visible in his face. It is much thinner and the former healthy tan has faded to a sallow pallor. Puffy shadows of sleeplessness and dissipation are marked under his heavy-lidded* .*)

*eyes. He is dressed in a well-fitting,
expensive dark suit, a white shirt with
a soft collar and bright-coloured tie.)*

MISS HOWARD (*with pleased surprise, holding out
her hand*). Hello, Mr. Murray.

MURRAY (*shaking her hand—with a forced pleasantness*).
How are you, Miss Howard?

MISS HOWARD. Fine as ever. It certainly looks
natural to see you around here again—not that I
hope you're here to stay, though. (*With a smile.*)
I suppose you're on your way to Eileen now. Well,
I won't keep you. I've stacks of work to do. (*She
opens the hall door. He starts for the porch.*) Oh, I
was forgetting—Congratulations! I've read those
stories—all of us have. They're great. We're all
so proud of you. You're one of our graduates, you
know.

MURRAY (*indifferently*). Oh,—that stuff.

MISS HOWARD (*gaily*). Don't be so modest. Well,
see you later, I hope.

MURRAY. Yes. Doctor Stanton invited me to
stay for supper and I may——

MISS HOWARD. Fine! Be sure to!

> (*She goes out. Murray walks to porch door
> and steps out. He finds Eileen's eyes
> waiting for him. As their eyes meet she
> gasps involuntarily and he stops short
> in his tracks. For a moment they remain
> looking at each other in silence.*)

EILEEN (*dropping her eyes—faintly*). Stephen.

121

MURRAY (*much moved, strides to her bedside and takes her hands awkwardly*). Eileen. (*Then after a second's pause, in which he searches her face and is shocked by the change illness has made—anxiously.*) How are you feeling, Eileen? (*He grows confused by her gaze and his eyes shift from hers, which search his face with wild yearning.*)

EILEEN (*forcing a smile*). Oh, I'm all right. (*Eagerly.*) But you, Stephen? How are you? (*Excitedly.*) Oh, it's good to see you again! (*Her eyes continue fixed on his face pleadingly, questioningly.*)

MURRAY (*haltingly*). And it's sure great to see you again, Eileen. (*He releases her hand and turns away.*) And I'm fine and dandy. I look a little done up, I guess, but that's only the result of too much New York.

EILEEN (*sensing from his manner that whatever she has hoped for from his visit is not to be, sinks back on the pillows, shutting her eyes hopelessly, and cannot control a sigh of pain.*)

MURRAY (*turning to her anxiously*). What's the matter, Eileen? You're not in pain, are you?

EILEEN (*wearily*). No.

MURRAY. You haven't been feeling badly lately, have you? Your letters suddenly stopped—not a line for the past three weeks—and I——

EILEEN (*bitterly*). I got tired of writing and never getting any answer, Stephen.

MURRAY (*shame-faced*). Come, Eileen, it wasn't

as bad as that. You'd think I never—and I did write, didn't I?

EILEEN. Right after you left here, you did, Stephen. Lately——

MURRAY. I'm sorry, Eileen. It wasn't that I didn't mean to—but—in New York it's so hard. You start to do one thing and something else interrupts you. You never seem to get any one thing done when it ought to be. You can understand that, can't you, Eileen?

EILEEN (*sadly*). Yes. I understand everything now.

MURRAY (*offended*). What do you mean by every-thing? You said that so strangely. You mean you don't believe—— (*But she remains silent with her eyes shut. He frowns and takes to pacing up and down beside the bed.*) Why have they got you stuck out here on this isolation porch, Eileen?

EILEEN (*dully*). There was no room on the main porch, I suppose.

MURRAY. You never mentioned in any of your letters——

EILEEN. It's not very cheerful to get letters full of sickness. I wouldn't like to, I know.

MURRAY (*hurt*). That isn't fair, Eileen. You know I—— How long have you been back in the In-firmary?

EILEEN. About a month.

MURRAY (*shocked*). A month! But you were up and about—on exercise, weren't you—before that?

123

EILEEN. No. I had to stay in bed while I was at the cottage.

MURRAY. You mean—ever since that time they sent you back—the day before I left?

EILEEN. Yes.

MURRAY. But I thought from the cheery tone of your letters that you were——

EILEEN (*uneasily*). Getting better? I am, Stephen. I'm strong enough to be up now, but Doctor Stanton wants me to take a good long rest this time so that when I do get up again I'll be sure—— (*She breaks off impatiently.*) But don't let's talk about it. I'm all right. (*Murray glances down at her face worriedly. She changes the subject.*) You've been over to see Doctor Stanton, haven't you?

MURRAY. Yes.

EILEEN. Did he examine you?

MURRAY. Yes. (*Carelessly.*) Oh, he found me O.K. I'm fine and dandy, as I said before.

EILEEN. I'm glad, Stephen. (*After a pause.*) Tell about yourself—what you've been doing. You've written a lot lately, haven't you?

MURRAY (*frowning*). No. I haven't been able to get down to it—somehow. There's so little time to yourself once you get to know people in New York. The sale of the stories you typed put me on easy street as far as money goes, so I've felt no need—— (*He laughs weakly.*) I guess I'm one of those who have to get down to hard pan before they get the kick to drive them to hard work.

124

EILEEN (*surprised*). Was it hard work writing them up here ? You used to seem so happy just in doing them.

MURRAY. I was—happier than I've been before or afterwards. (*Cynically.*) But—I don't know— it was a new game to me then and I was chuck full of illusions about the glory of it. (*He laughs half-heartedly.*) Now I'm hardly a bit more enthusiastic over it than I used to be over newspaper work. It's like everything else, I guess. When you've got it, you find you don't want it.

EILEEN (*looking at him wonderingly—disturbed*). But isn't just the writing itself worth while ?

MURRAY (*as if suddenly ashamed of himself—quickly*) Yes. Of course it is. I'm talking like a fool. I'm sore at everything because I'm dissatisfied with my own cussedness and laziness—and I want to pass the buck. (*With a smile of cheerful confidence.*) It's only a fit. I'll come out of it all right and get down to brass tacks again.

EILEEN (*with an encouraging smile*). That's the way you ought to feel. It'd be wrong—I've read the two stories that have come out so far over and over. They're fine, I think. Every line in them sounds like you, and at the same time sounds natural and like people and things you see every day. Everybody thinks they're fine, Stephen.

MURRAY (*pleased, but pretending cynicism*). Then they must be rotten. (*Then with self-assurance*). Well, I've plenty more of those stories in my head. Every time I think of my home town there seems to

125

be a new story in someone I've known there. (*Spiritedly.*) Oh, I'll pound them out some time when the spirit moves; and I'll make them so much better than what I've done so far, you won't recognise them. I feel it's in me to do it. (*Smiling.*) Darn it, do you know just talking about it makes me feel as if I could sit right down now and start in on one. Is it the fact I've worked here before—or is it seeing you, Eileen. (*Gratefully.*) I really believe it's you. I haven't forgotten how you helped me before.

EILEEN (*in a tone of pain*). Don't, Stephen. I didn't do anything.

MURRAY (*eagerly*). Yes, you did. You made it possible. I can't tell you what a help you were. And since I've left the San, I've looked forward to your letters to boost up my spirits. When I felt down in the mouth over my own idiocy, I used to re-read them, and they always were good medicine. I can't tell you how grateful I've felt, honestly!

EILEEN (*faintly*). You're kind to say so, Stephen —but it was nothing, really.

MURRAY. And I can't tell you how I've missed those letters for the past three weeks. They left a big hole in things. I was worried about you—not having heard a word. (*With a smile.*) So I came to look you up.

EILEEN (*faintly. Forcing an answering smile*). Well, you see now I'm all right.

MURRAY (*concealing his doubt*). Yes, of course you are. Only I'd a darn sight rather see you up and about. We could take a walk, then—through the woods. (*A wince of pain shadows Eileen's face. She closes her eyes. Murray continues softly, after a pause.*) You haven't forgotten that last night—out there—Eileen ?

EILEEN (*her lips trembling—trying to force a laugh*). Please don't remind me of that, Stephen. I was so silly and so sick, too. My temp was so high it must have made me—completely crazy—or I'd never dreamed of doing such a stupid thing. My head must have been full of wheels because I don't remember anything I did or said, hardly.

MURRAY (*his pride taken down a peg by this—in a hurt tone*). Oh! Well—I haven't forgotten and I never will, Eileen. (*Then his face clears up as if a weight had been taken off his conscience.*) Well—I rather thought you wouldn't take it seriously—afterwards. You were all up in the air that night. And you never mentioned it in your letters——

EILEEN (*pleadingly*). Don't talk about it ! Forget it ever happened. It makes me feel— (*with a half-hysterical laugh*)—like a fool !

MURRAY (*worried*). All right, Eileen. I won't. Don't get worked up over nothing. That isn't resting, you know. (*Looking down at her closed eyes—solicitously.*) Perhaps all my talking has tired you out ? Do you feel done up ? Why don't you try and take a nap now ?

EILEEN (*dully*). Yes, I'd like to sleep.

MURRAY (*clasps her hands gently*). I'll leave you

then. I'll drop back to say good-bye and stay awhile before I go. I won't leave until the last train. (*As she doesn't answer.*) Do you hear, Eileen?

EILEEN (*weakly*). Yes. You'll come back—to say good-bye.

MURRAY. Yes. I'll be back sure.

> (*He presses her hand and after a kindly glance of sympathy down at her face, tiptoes to the door and goes into the room, shutting the door behind him. When she hears the door shut Eileen struggles up in bed and stretches her arms after him with an agonised sob " Stephen ! " She hides her face in her hands and sobs brokenly. Murray walks across to the hall door and is about to go out when the door is opened and Miss Gilpin enters.*)

MISS GILPIN (*hurriedly*). How do you do, Mr. Murray. Doctor Stanton just told me you were here.

MURRAY (*as they shake hands—smiling*). How are you, Miss Gilpin?

MISS GILPIN. He said he'd examined you, and that you were O.K. I'm glad. (*Glancing at him keenly.*) You've been talking to Eileen?

MURRAY. Just left her this second. She wanted to sleep for a while.

MISS GILPIN (*wonderingly*). Sleep? (*Then hurriedly.*) It's too bad. I wish I'd known you were here sooner. I wanted very much to talk to you before you saw Eileen. You see, I knew you'd pay us a visit some time. (*With a worried smile.*) I still think I ought to have a talk with you.

MURRAY. Certainly, Miss Gilpin.

MISS GILPIN (*takes a chair and places it near the hall door*). Sit down. She can't hear us here. Goodness knows this is hardly the place for confidences, but there are visitors all over and it'll have to do. Did you close the door tightly? She mustn't hear me above all. (*She goes to the porch door and peeps out for a moment; then comes back to him with flashing eyes.*) She's crying! What have you been saying to her? Oh, it's too late, I know! The fools shouldn't have permitted you to see her before I—— What has happened out there? Tell me! I must know.

MURRAY (*stammering*). Happened? Nothing. She's crying? Why, Miss Gilpin—you know I wouldn't hurt her for worlds.

MISS GILPIN (*more calmly*). Intentionally. I know you wouldn't. But something has happened. (*Then briskly.*) We're talking at cross purposes. Since you don't seem inclined to confide in me, I'll have to in you. You noticed how badly she looks, didn't you?

MURRAY. Yes, I did.

MISS GILPIN (*gravely*). She's been going down hill steadily—(*meaningly*)—ever since you left. She's in a very serious state, let me impress you with that. We've all loved her, and felt so sorry for her and admired her spirit so—that's the only reason she's

129

been allowed to stay here so long after her time. We've kept hoping she'd start to pick up—in another day—in another week. But now that's all over. Doctor Stanton has given up hope of her improving here, and her father is unwilling to pay for her elsewhere now he knows there's a cheaper place—the State Farm. So she's to be sent there in a day or so.

MURRAY (*springing to his feet—horrified*). To the State Farm!

MISS GILPIN. Her time here is long past. You know the rule—and she isn't getting better.

MURRAY (*appalled*). That means——!

MISS GILPIN (*forcibly*). Death! That's what it means for her!

MURRAY (*stunned*). Good God, I never dreamed——

MISS GILPIN. With others it might be different. They might improve under changed surroundings. In her case, it's certain. She'll die. And it wouldn't do any good to keep her here, either. She'd die here. She'll die anywhere. She'll die because lately she's given up hope, she hasn't wanted to live any more. She's let herself go—and now it's too late.

MURRAY. Too late? You mean there's no chance—now? (*Miss Gilpin nods. Murray is overwhelmed—after a pause—stammering.*) Isn't there—anything—we can do?

MISS GILPIN (*sadly*). I don't know. I should have talked to you before you—— You see, she's seen you now. She knows. (*As he looks mystified she*

130

continues slowly.) I suppose you know that Eileen loves you, don't you?

MURRAY (*as if defending himself against an accusation—with confused alarm*). No—Miss Gilpin. You're wrong, honestly. She may have felt something like that—once—but that was long ago before I left the San. She's forgotten all about it since, I know she has. (*Miss Gilpin smiles bitterly.*) Why, she never even alluded to it in any of her letters—all these months.

MISS GILPIN. Did you in yours?

MURRAY. No, of course not. You don't understand. Why—just now—she said that part of it had all been so silly she felt she'd acted like a fool and didn't ever want to be reminded of it.

MISS GILPIN. She saw that you didn't love her—any more than you did in the days before you left. Oh, I used to watch you then. I sensed what was going on between you. I would have stopped it then out of pity for her, if I could have, if I didn't know that any interference would only make matters worse. And then I thought that it might be only a surface affair—that after you were gone it would end for her. (*She sighs—then after a pause.*) You'll have to forgive me for speaking to you so boldly on a delicate subject. But, don't you see, it's for her sake. I love Eileen. We all do. (*Averting her eyes from his—in a low voice.*) I know how Eileen feels, ﬞMr. Murray. Once—a long time ago—I suffered as she is suffering—from this same mistake. But I had resources to fall back upon that Eileen

131

hasn't got—a family who loved me and understood —friends—so I pulled through. But it spoiled my life for a long time. (*Looking at him again and forcing a smile.*) So I feel that perhaps I have a right to speak for Eileen who has no one else.

MURRAY (*huskily—much moved*). Say anything to me you like, Miss Gilpin.

MISS GILPIN (*after a pause—sadly*). You don't love her—do you?

MURRAY. No—I—— I don't believe I've ever thought much of loving anyone—that way.

MISS GILPIN (*sadly*). Oh, it's too late, I'm afraid. If we had only had this talk before you had seen her! I meant to talk to you frankly and if I found out you didn't love Eileen—there was always the forlorn hope that you might—I was going to tell you not to see her, for her sake—not to let her face the truth. For I am sure she continued to hope in spite of everything, and always would—to the end—if she didn't see you. I was going to implore you to stay away, to write her letters that would encourage her hope, and in that way she would never learn the truth. I thought of writing you all this—but—it's so delicate a matter—I didn't have the courage. (*With intense grief.*) And now Doctor Stanton's decision to send her away makes everything doubly hard. When she knows *that*—she will throw everything that holds her to life—out of the window! And think of it— her dying there alone!

MURRAY (*very pale*). Don't! That shan't happen. I can at least save her from that. I have money enough—I'll make more—to send her to any place you think——

MISS GILPIN. That is something—but it doesn't touch the source of her unhappiness. If there were only some way to make her happy in the little time that is left to her! She has suffered so much through you. Oh, Mr. Murray, can't you tell her you love her?

MURRAY (*after a pause—slowly*). But she'll never believe me, I'm afraid, now.

MISS GILPIN (*eagerly*). But you must make her believe! And you must ask her to marry you. If you're engaged it will give you the right in her eyes to take her away. You can take her to some private San. There's a small place, but a very good one, at White Lake. It's not too expensive, and it's a beautiful spot, out of the world, and you can live and work near by. And she'll be happy to the very last. Don't you think that's something—the best you have—the best you can give in return for her love for you?

MURRAY (*slowly — deeply moved*). Yes. (*Then determinedly.*) But I won't go into this thing by halves. It isn't fair to her. I'm going to marry her—yes, I mean it. I owe her that if it will make her happy. But to ask her without really meaning it—knowing she—no, I can't do that.

MISS GILPIN (*with a sad smile*). I'm glad you feel that way. It shouldn't be hard now for you to convince her. But I know Eileen. She will never consent—for your sake—until she is well again. And

133

stop and think, Mr. Murray. Even if she did consent to marry you right now the shock—the excitement—it would be suicide for her. I would have to warn her against it myself; and you wouldn't propose it if you knew the danger to her in her present condition. She hasn't long to live, at best. I've talked with Dr. Stanton. I know. God knows I would be the first one to hold out hope if there was any. There isn't. It's merely a case of prolonging the short time left to her and making it happy. You must bear that in mind—as a fact!

MURRAY (*dully*). All right. I'll remember. But it's hell to realise—— (*He turns suddenly towards the porch door.*) I'll go out to her now while I feel—that —yes, I know I can make her believe me now.

MISS GILPIN. You'll tell me—later on?

MURRAY. Yes. (*He opens the door to the porch and goes out. Miss Gilpin stands for a moment looking after him worriedly. Then she sighs helplessly and goes out to the hall. Murray steps noiselessly out on the porch. Eileen is lying motionless with her eyes closed. Murray stands looking at her, his face showing the emotional stress he is under, a great pitying tenderness in his eyes. Then he seems to come to a revealing decision on what is best to do for he tiptoes to the bedside and bending down with a quick movement, takes her in his arms and kisses her.*) Eileen!

EILEEN (*startled at first, resists automatically for a moment*). Stephen! (*Then she succumbs and lies back in his arms with a happy sigh, putting both hands*
134

to the sides of his face and staring up at him adoringly.)
Stephen, dear !

MURRAY (*quickly questioning her before she can question him*). You were fibbing—about that night —weren't you ? You do love me, don't you, Eileen ?

EILEEN (*breathlessly*). Yes—I—but you, Stephen —you don't love me. (*She makes a movement as if to escape from his embrace.*)

MURRAY (*genuinely moved—with tender reassurance*). Why do you suppose I came up here if not to tell you I did ? But they warned me—Miss Gilpin —that you were still weak and that I mustn't excite you in any way. And I—I didn't want—but I had to come back and tell you in spite of them.

EILEEN (*convinced—with a happy laugh*). And is that why you acted so strange—and cold ? Aren't they silly to tell you that ! As if being happy could hurt me ! Why, it's just that, just you I've needed !

MURRAY (*his voice trembling*). And you'll marry me, Eileen ?

EILEEN (*a shadow of doubt crossing her face momentarily*). Are you sure—you want me, Stephen ?

MURRAY (*a lump in his throat—huskily*). Yes. I do want you, Eileen.

EILEEN (*happily*). Then I will—after I'm well again, of course. (*She kisses him.*)

MURRAY (*chokingly*). That won't be long now, Eileen.

EILEEN (*joyously*). No—not long—now that I'm happy for once in my life. I'll surprise you, Stephen,

135

the way I'll pick up and grow fat and healthy. You won't know me in a month. How can you ever love such a skinny homely thing as I am now! (*With a laugh.*) I couldn't if I was a man—love such a fright.

MURRAY. Ssshh!

EILEEN (*confidently*). But you'll see now. I'll make myself get well. We won't have to wait long, dear. And can't you move up to the town near here where you can see me every day, and you can work and I can help you with your stories just as I used to—and I'll soon be strong enough to do your typing again. (*She laughs.*) Listen to me—talking about helping you—as if they weren't all your own work, those blessed stories!—as if I had anything to do with it!

MURRAY (*hoarsely*). You had! You did! They're yours. (*Trying to calm himself.*) But you mustn't stay here, Eileen. You'll let me take you away, won't you? —to a better place—not far away—White Lake, it's called. There's a small private sanatorium there. Doctor Stanton says it's one of the best. And I'll live near by—it's a beautiful spot—and see you every day.

EILEEN (*in the seventh heaven*). And did you plan out all this for me beforehand, Stephen? (*He nods with averted eyes. She kisses his hair.*) You wonderful, kind dear! And it's a small place—this White Lake? Then we won't have so many people around to disturb us, will we? We'll be all to ourselves. And you ought to work so well up there. I know New York wasn't good for you—alone—without me. And I'll get well and strong so quick! And you say it's a beautiful place? (*Intensely.*) Oh, Stephen,

136

any place in the world would be beautiful to me—if you were with me! (*His face is hidden in the pillow beside her. She is suddenly startled by a muffled sob—anxiously.*) Why—Stephen—you're—you're crying! (*The tears start to her own eyes.*)

MURRAY (*raising his face which is this time alight with a passionate awakening—a revelation*). Oh, I do love you, Eileen. I do! I love you, love you!

EILEEN (*thrilled by the depth of his present sincerity—but with a teasing laugh*). Why, you say that as if you'd just made the discovery, Stephen!

MURRAY. Oh, what does it matter, Eileen! I love you! Oh, what a blind, selfish ass I've been! I love you! You are my life—everything! I love you, Eileen! I do! I do! And we'll be married——

> (*Suddenly his face grows frozen with horror as he remembers the doom. For the first time the grey spectre of Death confronts him face to face as a menacing reality.*)

EILEEN (*terrified by the look in his eyes*). What is it, Stephen? What——?

MURRAY (*with a groan—protesting half-aloud in a strangled voice*). No! No! It can't be——! My God! (*He clutches her hands and hides his face in them.*)

EILEEN (*with a cry*). Stephen! What is the matter? (*Her face suddenly betrays apprehension, an intuitive sense of the truth.*) Oh—Stephen—— (*Then with a childish whimper of terror.*) Oh, Stephen, I'm going to die! I'm going to die!

MURRAY (*lifting his tortured face—wildly*). No!

137

EILEEN (*her voice sinking to a dead whisper*). I'm going to die.

MURRAY (*seizing her in his arms in a passionate frenzy and pressing his lips to hers*). No, Eileen, no, my love, no! What are you saying? What could have made you think it? You—die? Why, of course, we're all going to die—but—Good God! What damned nonsense! You're getting well— every day. Everyone — Miss Gilpin — Stanton — everyone told me that. I swear before God, Eileen, they did! You're still weak, that's all. They said —it won't be long. You mustn't think that—not now.

EILEEN (*miserably—unconvinced*). But why did you look at me—that way—with that awful look in your eyes——?

> (*While she is speaking Miss Gilpin enters the room from the corridor. She appears worried, agitated. She hurries towards the porch, but stops inside the doorway, arrested by Murray's voice.*)

MURRAY (*takes Eileen by the shoulders and forces her to look into his eyes*). I wasn't thinking about you then—— No, Eileen—not you. I didn't mean you—but me—yes, me! I couldn't tell you before. They'd warned me—not to excite you—and I knew that would—if you loved me.

EILEEN (*staring at him with frightened amazement*). You mean you—— you're sick again?

MURRAY (*desperately striving to convince her*). Yes. I saw Stanton. I lied to you before—about that. It's come back on me, Eileen—you see how I look—

I've let myself go. I don't know how to live without you, don't you see? And you'll—marry me now —without waiting—and help me to get well—you and I together—and not mind their lies—what they say to prevent you? You'll do that, Eileen?

EILEEN. I'll do anything for you—— And I'd be so happy—— (*She breaks down.*) But, Stephen, I'm so afraid. I'm all mixed up. Oh, Stephen, I don't know what to believe!

MISS GILPIN (*who has been listening thunderstruck to Murray's wild pleading, at last summons up the determination to interfere—steps out on the porch— in a tone of severe remonstrance*). Mr. Murray!

MURRAY (*starts to his feet with wild, bewildered eyes—confusedly*). Oh—you—— (*Miss Gilpin cannot restrain an exclamation of dismay as she sees his face wrung by despair. Eileen turns her head away with a little cry, as if she would hide her face in the bedclothes. A sudden fierce resolution lights up Murray's countenance—hoarsely.*) You're just in the nick of time, Miss Gilpin! Eileen! Listen! You'll believe Miss Gilpin, won't you? She knows all about it. (*Eileen turns her eyes questioningly on the bewildered nurse.*)

MISS GILPIN. What——?

MURRAY (*determinedly*). Miss Gilpin, Doctor Stanton has spoken to you since he examined me. He must have told you the truth about me. Eileen doesn't believe me—when I tell her I've got T. B. again. She thinks—I don't know what. I know you're not supposed to, but can't you make an exception—in this case? Can't you tell Eileen the truth?

139

MISS GILPIN (*stunned by being thus defiantly confronted—stammeringly*). Mr. Murray! I—I—how can you ask——

MURRAY (*quickly*). Eileen has a right to know. She loves me—and I—I—love her! (*He holds her eyes and speaks with a passion of sincerity that compels belief.*) I love her, do you hear?

MISS GILPIN (*falteringly*). You—love—Eileen?

MURRAY. Yes! I do! (*Entreatingly.*) So—tell her—won't you?

MISS GILPIN (*swallowing hard, her eyes full of pity and sorrow fixed on Eileen*). Yes—Eileen—it's true. (*She turns away slowly towards the door.*)

EILEEN (*with a little cry of alarmed concern, stretches out her hands to Murray protectingly*). Poor Stephen—dear! (*He grasps her hands and kisses them.*)

MISS GILPIN (*in a low voice*). Mr. Murray. May I speak to you for a moment?

MURRAY (*with a look of questioning defiance at her*). Certainly.

MISS GILPIN (*turns to Eileen with a forced smile*). I won't steal him away for more than a moment, Eileen. (*Eileen smiles happily.*)

MURRAY (*follows Miss Gilpin into the room. She leads him to the far end of the room near the door to the hall, after shutting the porch door carefully behind him. He looks at her defiantly*). Well?

MISS GILPIN (*in low agitated tones*). What has happened? What is the meaning—I feel as if I may have done a great wrong to myself—to you—to her—by that lie. And yet—something impelled me.

140

MURRAY (*moved*). Don't regret it, Miss Gilpin! It has saved her—us. Oh, how can I explain what happened? I suddenly saw—how beautiful and sweet and good she is—how I couldn't bear the thought of life without her—her love—— That's all. (*Determinedly.*) She must marry me at once and I will take her away—the far West—any place Stanton thinks can help. And she can take care of me—as she thinks—and I know she will grow well as I seem to grow well. Oh Miss Gilpin, don't you see? No half and half measures—no promises—no conditional engagements—can help us—help her. We love too much! (*Fiercely, as if defying her.*) But we'll win together. We can! We must! There are things your doctors cannot value—cannot know the strength of! (*Exultantly.*) You'll see! I'll make Eileen get well, I tell you! Happiness will cure! Love is stronger than—— (*He suddenly breaks down before the pitying negation she cannot keep from her eyes. He sinks on a chair, shoulders bowed, face hidden in his hands, with a groan of despair.*) Oh, why did you give me a hopeless hope?

MISS GILPIN (*putting her hand on his shoulder—with tender compassion—sadly*). Isn't everything we know—just that—when you think of it? (*Her face lighting up with a consoling revelation.*) But there must be something behind it—some promise of fulfilment, — somehow — somewhere — in the spirit of hope itself.

MURRAY (*dully*). Yes—but what do words mean to me now? (*Then suddenly starting to his feet and flinging off her hand with disdainful strength—violently and almost insultingly.*) What damned rot! I tell you we'll win! We must! Oh, I'm a fool to waste words on you! What can you know? Love isn't in the materia medica. Your predictions—all the verdicts of all the doctors—what do they matter to me? This is—beyond you! And we'll win in spite of you! (*Scornfully.*) How dare you use the word hopeless—as if it were the last! Come now, confess, damn it! There's always hope, isn't there? What do you *know?* Can you say you *know* anything?

MISS GILPIN (*taken aback by his violence for a moment, finally bursts into a laugh of helplessness which is close to tears*). I? I know nothing—absolutely nothing! God bless you both!

> (*She raises her handkerchief to her eyes and hurries out to the corridor without turning her head. Murray stands looking after her for a moment; then strides out to the porch.*)

EILEEN (*turning and greeting him with a shy smile of happiness as he comes and kneels by her bedside*). Stephen! (*He kisses her. She strokes his hair and continues in a tone of motherly, self-forgetting solicitude.*) I'll have to look out for you, Stephen, won't I? From now on? And see that you rest so many hours a day—and drink your milk when I drink mine—and go to bed at nine sharp when I do—and obey everything I tell you—and——

THE CURTAIN FALLS

The Emperor Jones

Characters

BRUTUS JONES, *Emperor.*

HENRY SMITHERS, *A Cockney Trader.*

AN OLD NATIVE WOMAN.

LEM, *A Native Chief.*

SOLDIERS, *Adherents of Lem.*

The Little Formless Fears; Jeff; The Negro Convicts; The Prison Guard; The Planters; The Auctioneer; The Slaves; The Congo Witch-Doctor; The Crocodile God.

The action of the play takes place on an island in the West Indies as yet not self-determined by White Mariners. The form of native government is, for the time being, an Empire.

Scene One

The audience chamber in the palace of the Emperor—a spacious, high-ceilinged room with bare, white-washed walls. The floor is of white tiles. In the rear, to the left of centre, a wide archway giving out on a portico with white pillars. The palace is evidently situated on high ground for beyond the portico nothing can be seen but a vista of distant hills, their summits crowned with thick groves of palm trees. In the right wall, centre, a smaller arched doorway leading to the living quarters of the palace. The room is bare of furniture with the exception of one huge chair made of uncut wood which stands at centre, its back to rear. This is very apparently the Emperor's throne. It is painted a dazzling, eye-smiting scarlet. There is a brilliant orange cushion on the seat and another smaller one is placed on the floor to serve as a foot-stool. Strips of matting, dyed scarlet, lead from the foot of the throne to the two entrances.

It is late afternoon, but the yellow sunlight still blazes beyond the portico and there is an oppressive burden of exhausting heat in the air.

As the curtain rises, a native negro woman

147

sneaks in cautiously from the entrance on the right. She is very old, dressed in cheap calico, bare-footed, a red bandana handkerchief covering all but a few stray wisps of white hair. A bundle bound in coloured cloth is carried over her shoulder on the end of a stick. She hesitates beside the doorway, peering back as if in extreme dread of being discovered. Then she begins to glide noiselessly, a step at a time, towards the doorway in the rear. At this moment Smithers appears beneath the portico.

Smithers is a tall man, round-shouldered, about forty. His bald head, perched on a long neck with an enormous Adam's apple, looks like an egg. The tropics have tanned his naturally pasty face with its small, sharp features to a sickly yellow, and native rum has painted his pointed nose to a startling red. His little washy-blue eyes are red-rimmed and dart about him like a ferret's. His expression is one of unscrupulous meanness, cowardly and dangerous. He is dressed in a worn riding suit of dirty white drill, puttees, spurs, and wears a white cork helmet. A cartridge belt with an automatic revolver is around his waist. He carries a riding whip in his hand. He sees the woman and stops to watch her suspiciously. Then, making up his mind, he steps quickly on tiptoe into the room. The woman, looking back over her shoulder continually, does not see him until it is too late. When she does Smithers springs forward and grabs her firmly by the shoulder. She struggles to get away, fiercely but silently.

SMITHERS (*tightening his grasp—roughly*). Easy!

148

None o' that, me birdie. You can't wriggle out now.
I got me 'ooks on yer.

WOMAN (*seeing the uselessness of struggling, gives way to
frantic terror, and sinks to the ground, embracing his
knees supplicatingly*). No tell him! No tell him,
Mister!

SMITHERS (*with great curiosity*). Tell 'im? (*Then
scornfully.*) Oh, you mean 'is bloomin' Majesty.
What's the game, any 'ow? What are you sneakin'
away for? Been stealin' a bit, I s'pose. (*He taps
her bundle with his riding whip significantly.*)

WOMAN (*shaking her head vehemently*). No, me
no steal.

SMITHERS. Bloody liar! But tell me what's up.
There's somethin' funny goin' on. I smelled it in
the air first thing I got up this mornin'. You blacks
are up to some devilment. This palace of 'is is like
a bleedin' tomb. Where's all the 'ands? (*The woman
keeps sullenly silent. Smithers raises his whip
threateningly.*) Ow, yer won't, won't yer? I'll
show yer what's what.

WOMAN (*coweringly*). I tell, Mister. You no hit.
They go—all go. (*She makes a sweeping gesture
towards the hills in the distance.*)

SMITHERS. Run away—to the 'ills?

WOMAN. Yes, Mister. Him Emperor—Great
Father. (*She touches her forehead to the floor with a
quick mechanical jerk.*) Him sleep after eat. Then
they go—all go. Me old woman. Me left only.
Now me go too.

SMITHERS (*his astonishment giving way to an immense,*

mean satisfaction). Ow! So that's the ticket! Well,
I know bloody well wot's in the air—when they runs
orf to the 'ills. The tom-tom 'll be thumping out
there bloomin' soon. (*With extreme vindictiveness.*)
And I'm bloody glad of it, for one! Serve 'im right!
Puttin' on airs, the stinkin' nigger! 'Is Majesty!
Gawd blimey! I only hopes I'm there when they
takes 'im out to shoot 'im. (*Suddenly.*) 'E's still 'ere
all right, ain't 'e?

WOMAN. Yes. Him sleep.

SMITHERS. 'E's bound to find out soon as 'e wakes
up. 'E's cunnin' enough to know when 'is time's
come. (*He goes to the doorway on right and whistles
shrilly with his fingers in his mouth. The old woman
springs to her feet and runs out of the doorway, rear.
Smithers goes after her, reaching for his revolver.*)
Stop or I'll shoot! (*Then stooping—indifferently.*)
Pop orf then, if yer like, yer black cow. (*He stands
in the doorway, looking after her.*)

> (*Jones enters from the right. He is a tall,
> powerfully-built, full-blooded negro of
> middle age. His features are typically
> negroid, yet there is something decidedly
> distinctive about his face—an underlying
> strength of will, a hardy, self-reliant con-
> fidence in himself that inspires respect.
> His eyes are alive with a keen, cunning
> intelligence. In manner he is shrewd,
> suspicious, evasive. He wears a light
> blue uniform coat, sprayed with brass
> buttons, heavy gold chevrons on his shoulders,*

150

*gold braid on the collar, cuffs, etc. His
trousers are bright red with a light blue
stripe down the side. Patent leather
laced boots with brass spurs, and a belt
with a long-barrelled, pearl-handled
revolver in a holster complete his attire.
Yet there is something not altogether
ridiculous about his grandeur. He has a
way of carrying it off.*)

JONES (*not seeing anyone—greatly irritated and blinking
sleepily—shouts*). Who dare whistle dat way in my
palace ? Who dare wake up de Emperor ? I'll git
de hide flayed off some o' you niggers sho' !

SMITHERS (*showing himself—in a manner half-afraid
and half-defiant*). It was me whistled to yer. (*As
Jones frowns angrily.*) I got news for yer.

JONES (*putting on his suavest manner, which fails
to cover up his contempt for the white man.*) Oh, it's
you, Mister Smithers. (*He sits down on his throne
with easy dignity.*) What news you got to tell me ?

SMITHERS (*coming close to enjoy his discomfiture*).
Don't yer notice nothin' funny to-day ?

JONES (*coldly*). Funny ? No. I ain't perceived
nothin' of de kind !

SMITHERS. Then yer ain't so foxy as I thought yer
was. Where's all your court ? (*Sarcastically.*) The
Generals and the Cabinet Ministers and all ?

JONES (*imperturbably*). Where dey mostly runs to
minute I closes my eyes—drinkin' rum and talkin' big
down in de town. (*Sarcastically.*) How come you

don't know dat? Ain't you carousing with 'em most every day?

SMITHERS (*stung, but pretending indifference—with a wink*). That's part of the day's work. I got ter—ain't I—in my business?

JONES (*contemptuously*). Yo' business!

SMITHERS (*imprudently enraged*). Gawd blimey, you was glad enough for me ter take yer in on it when you landed here first. You didn't 'ave no 'igh and mighty airs in them days!

JONES (*his hand going to his revolver like a flash—menacingly*). Talk polite, white man! Talk polite, you heah me! I'm boss heah now, is you fergettin'?

> (*The Cockney seems about to challenge this last statement with the facts, but something in the other's eyes holds and cowers him.*)

SMITHERS (*in a cowardly whine*). No 'arm meant, old top.

JONES (*condescendingly*). I accepts yo' apology. (*Lets his hand fall from his revolver.*) No use'n you rakin' up ole times. What I was den is one thing. What I is now 's another. You didn't let me in on yo' crooked work out o' no kind feelin's dat time. I done de dirty work fo' you—and most o' de brain work, too, fo' dat matter—and I was wu'th money to you, dat's de reason.

SMITHERS. Well, blimey, I give yer a start, didn't I—when no one else would. I wasn't afraid to 'ire yer like the rest was—'count of the story about your breakin' jail back in the States.

JONES. No, you didn't have no s'cuse to look down on me fo' dat. You been in jail you'self more'n once.

SMITHERS (*furiously*). It's a lie! (*Then trying to pass it off by an attempt at scorn*). Garn! Who told yer that fairy tale?

JONES. Dey's some tings I ain't got to be tole. I kin see 'em in folk's eyes. (*Then after a pause—meditatively.*) Yes, you sho' give me a start. And it didn't take long from dat time to git dese fool woods' niggers right where I wanted dem. (*With pride.*) From stowaway to Emperor in two years! Dat's goin' some!

SMITHERS (*with curiosity*). And I bet you got yer pile o' money 'id safe some place.

JONES (*with satisfaction*). I sho' has! And it's in a foreign bank where no pusson don't ever git it out but me no matter what come. You didn't s'pose I was holdin' down dis Emperor job for de glory in it, did you? Sho'! De fuss and glory part of it, dat's only to turn de heads o' de low-flung bush niggers dat's here. Dey wants de big circus show for deir money. I gives it to 'em an' I gits de money. (*With a grin.*) De long green, dat's me every time! (*Then rebukingly.*) But you ain't got no kick agin me, Smithers. I'se paid you back all you done for me many times. Ain't I pertected you and winked at all de crooked tradin' you been doin' right out in de broad day. Sho' I has—and me makin' laws to stop it at de same time! (*He chuckles.*)

SMITHERS (*grinning*). But, meanin' no' 'arm, you
153

been grabbin' right and left yourself, ain't yer? Look at the taxes you've put on 'em! Blimey! You've squeezed 'em dry!

JONES (*chuckling*). No, dey ain't *all* dry yet. I'se still heah, ain't I?

SMITHERS (*smiling at his secret thought.*) They're dry right now, you'll find out. (*Changing the subject abruptly.*) And as for me breakin' laws, you've broke 'em all yerself just as fast as yer made 'em.

JONES. Ain't I de Emperor? De laws don't go for him. (*Judicially.*) You heah what I tells you, Smithers. Dere's little stealin' like you does, and dere's big stealin' like I does. For de little stealin' dey gits you in jail soon or late. For de big stealin' dey makes you Emperor and puts you in de Hall o' Fame when you croaks. (*Reminiscently.*) If dey's one thing I learns in ten years on de Pullman ca's listenin' to de white quality talk, it's dat same fact. And when I gits a chance to use it I winds up Emperor in two years.

SMITHERS (*unable to repress the genuine admiration of the small fry for the large*). Yes, yer turned the bleedin' trick, all right. Blimey, I never seen a bloke 'as 'ad the bloomin' luck you 'as.

JONES (*severely*). Luck? What you mean—luck?

SMITHERS. I suppose you'll say as that swank about the silver bullet ain't luck—and that was what first got the fool blacks on yer side the time of the revolution, wasn't it?

JONES (*with a laugh*). Oh, dat silver bullet! Sho'

154

was luck! But I makes dat luck, you heah? I loads de dice! Yessuh! When dat murderin' nigger ole Lem hired to kill me takes aim ten feet away and his gun misses fire and I shoots him dead, what you heah me say?

SMITHERS. You said yer'd got a charm so's no lead bullet'd kill yer. You was so strong only a silver bullet could kill yer, you told 'em. Blimey, wasn't that swank for yer, and plain, fat-'eaded luck?

JONES (*proudly*). I got brains and I uses 'em quick. Dat ain't luck.

SMITHERS. Yer know they wasn't 'ardly liable to get no silver bullets. And it was luck 'e didn't 'it you that time.

JONES (*laughing*). And dere all dem fool bush niggers was kneelin' down and bumpin' deir heads on de ground like I was a miracle out o' de Bible. Oh Lawd, from dat time on I has dem all eatin' out of my hand. I cracks de whip and dey jumps through.

SMITHERS (*with a sniff*). Yankee bluff done it.

JONES. Ain't a man's talkin' big what makes him big—long as he makes folks believe it? Sho', I talks large when I ain't got nothin' to back it up, but I ain't talkin' wild just de same. I knows I kin fool 'em—I *knows* it—and dat's backin' enough fo' my game. And ain't I got to learn deir lingo and teach some of dem English befo' I kin talk to em? Ain't dat wuk? You ain't never learned any word of it, Smithers in de ten years you been heah, dough you' knows it's money in yo' pocket tradin' wid 'em if you does. But you'se too shiftless to take de trouble.

155

SMITHERS (*flushing*). Never mind about me. What's this I've 'eard about yer really 'avin' a silver bullet moulded for yourself?

JONES. It's playin' out my bluff. I has de silver bullet moulded and I tells 'em when de time comes I kills myself wid it. I tells 'em dat's 'cause I'm de on'y man in de world big enuff to git me. No use'n deir tryin'. And dey falls down and bumps deir heads. (*He laughs.*) I does dat so's I kin take a walk in peace widout no jealous nigger gunnin' at me from behind de trees.

SMITHERS (*astonished*). Then you 'ad it made— 'onest?

JONES. Sho' did. Heah she be. (*He takes out his revolver, breaks it, and takes the bullet out of one chamber.*) Five lead an' dis silver baby at de last. Don't she shine pretty? (*He holds it in his hand, looking at it admiringly, as if strangely fascinated.*)

SMITHERS. Let me see. (*Reaches out his hand for it.*)

JONES (*harshly*). Keep yo' hands whar dey b'long, white man. (*He replaces it in the chamber and puts the revolver back on his hip.*)

SMITHERS (*snarling*). Gawd blimey! Think I'm a bleedin' thief, you would.

JONES. No, 'tain't dat. I knows you'se scared to steal from me. On'y I ain't 'lowin' nary body to touch dis baby. She's my rabbit's foot.

SMITHERS (*sneering*). A bloomin' charm, wot?

(*Venomously.*) Well, you'll need all the bloody charms you 'as before long, s' 'elp me!

JONES (*judicially*). Oh, I'se good for six months yit 'fore dey gits sick o' my game. Den, when I sees trouble comin', I makes a move.

SMITHERS. Ho! You got it all planned, ain't yer?

JONES. I ain't no fool. I knows dis Emperor's time is sho't. Dat why I make hay when de sun shine. Was you thinkin' I'se aimin' to hold down dis job for life? No, suh! What good is gittin' money if you stays back in dis raggedy country? I wants action when I spends. And when I sees dese niggers gittin' up deir nerve to tu'n me out, and I'se got all de money in sight, I resigns on de spot and gets away quick.

SMITHERS. Where to?

JONES. None o' yo' business.

SMITHERS. Not back to the bloody States, I'll lay my oath.

JONES (*suspiciously*). Why don't I? (*Then with an easy laugh.*) You mean 'count of dat story 'bout me breakin' from jail back dere? Dat's all talk.

SMITHERS (*sceptically*). Ho, yes!

JONES (*sharply*). You ain't 'sinuatin' I'se a liar, is you?

SMITHERS (*hastily*). No, Gawd strike me! I was only thinkin' o' the bloody lies you told the blacks 'ere about killin' white men in the States.

157

JONES (*angered*). How come dey're lies ?

SMITHERS. You'd 'ave been in jail if you 'ad, wouldn't yer then ? (*With venom.*) And from what I've 'eard, it ain't 'ealthy for a black to kill a white man in the States. They burns 'em in oil, don't they ?

JONES (*with cool deadliness*). You mean lynchin' 'd scare me ? Well, I tells you, Smithers, maybe I does kill one white man back dere. Maybe I does. And maybe I kills another right heah 'fore long if he don't look out.

SMITHERS (*trying to force a laugh*). I was on'y spoofin' yer. Can't yer take a joke ? And you was just sayin' you'd never been in jail.

JONES (*in the same tone—slightly boastful*). Maybe I goes to jail dere for gettin' in an argument wid razors ovah a game of dice. Maybe I gits twenty years when dat coloured man die. Maybe I gits in 'nother argument wid de prison guard and de overseer ovah us when we're wukin' de roads. Maybe he hits me wid a whip and I splits his head wid a shovel and runs away and files de chain off my leg and gits away safe. Maybe I does all dat an' maybe I don't. It's a story I tells you so's you knows I'se de kind of man dat if you evah repeats one word of it, I ends yo' stealin' on dis yearth mighty damn quick !

SMITHERS (*terrified*). Think I'd peach on yer ? Not me ! Ain't I always been yer friend ?

JONES (*suddenly relaxing*). Sho' you has—and you better be.

SMITHERS (*recovering his composure—and with it his malice*). And just to show yer I'm yer friend, I'll tell yer that bit o' news I was goin' to.

JONES. Go ahead! Must be bad news from de happy way you look.

SMITHERS (*warningly*). Maybe it's gettin' time for you to resign—with that bloomin' silver bullet, wot? (*He finishes with a mocking grin.*)

JONES (*puzzled*). What's dat you say? Talk plain.

SMITHERS. Ain't noticed any of the guards or servants about the place to-day, I 'aven't.

JONES (*carelessly*). Dey're all out in de garden sleepin' under de trees. When I sleeps, dey sneaks a sleep too, and I pretends I never suspicions it. All I got to do is to ring de bell and dey come flyin', makin' a bluff dey was wukin' all de time.

SMITHERS (*in the same mocking tone*). Ring the bell now an' you'll bloody well see what I mean.

JONES (*startled to alertness, but preserving the same careless tone*). Sho' I rings.

> (*He reaches below the throne and pulls out a big common dinner bell which is painted the same vivid scarlet as the throne. He rings this vigorously—then stops to listen. Then he goes to both doors, rings again, and looks out.*)

SMITHERS (*watching him with malicious satisfaction, after a pause—mockingly*). The bloody ship is sinkin' an' the bleedin' rats 'as slung their 'ooks.

JONES (*in a sudden fit of anger flings the bell clattering into a corner*). Low-flung bush niggers! (*Then catching Smithers' eye on him, he controls himself and suddenly bursts into a low chuckling laugh.*) Reckon I overplays my hand dis once! A man can't take de pot on a short-tailed flush all de time. Was I sayin' I'd sit it six months mo'? Well, I'se changed my mind den. I gives in and resigns de job of Emperor right dis minute.

SMITHERS (*with real admiration*). Blimey, but you're a cool bird, and no mistake.

JONES. No use'n fussin'. When I knows de game's up I kisses it good-bye widout no long waits. Dey've all run off to de hills, ain't dey?

SMITHERS. Yes—every bleedin' man jack of 'em.

JONES. Den de revolution is at de door. And de Emperor better git his feet movin' up de trail. (*He starts for the door in rear.*)

SMITHERS. Goin' out to look for your 'orse? Yer won't find any. They steals the 'orses first thing. Mine was gone when I went for 'im this mornin'. That's wot first give me a suspicion of wot was up.

JONES (*alarmed for a second, scratches his head, then philosophically*). Well, den I hoofs it. Feet, do yo' duty! (*He pulls out a gold watch and looks at it.*) Three-thuty. Sundown's at six-thuty or dereabouts. (*Puts his watch back—with cool confidence.*) I got plenty o' time to make it easy.

SMITHERS. Don't be so bloomin' sure of it. They'll be after you 'ot and 'eavy. Ole Lem is at the bottom o' this business an' 'e 'ates you like 'ell. 'E'd rather do for you than eat 'is dinner, 'e would!

JONES (*scornfully*). Dat fool no-count nigger! Does you think I'se scared o' him? I stands him on his thick head more'n once befo' dis, and I does it again if he comes in my way—— (*Fiercely.*) And dis time I leave him a dead nigger fo' sho'!

SMITHERS. You'll 'ave to cut through the big forest—an' these blacks 'ere can sniff and follow a trail in the dark like 'ounds. You'd 'ave to 'ustle to get through that forest in twelve hours even if you knew all the bloomin' paths like a native.

JONES (*with indignant scorn*). Look-a-heah, white man! Does you think I'se a natural bo'n fool? Give me credit fo' havin' some sense, fo' Lawd's sake! Don't you s'pose I'se looked ahead and made sho' of all de chances? I'se gone out in dat big forest, pretendin' to hunt, so many times dat I knows it high an' low like a book. I could go through on dem paths wid my eyes shut. (*With great contempt.*) Think dese ig'nerent bush niggers dat ain't got brains enuff to know deir own names even, can catch Brutus Jones? Huh, I s'pects not! Not on yo' life! Why, man, de white men went after me wid bloodhounds, where I come from an' I jes' laughs at 'em. It's a shame to fool dese black trash around heah, dey're so easy. You watch me, man'. I'll make dem look sick, I will. I'll be 'cross de plain to de edge of de forest by time dark comes. Once in de woods in de night, dey got a fine chance o' findin' dis baby! Dawn to-morrow I'll be out at de oder side and on de coast whar dat French gunboat is stayin'. She picks me up, take me to the Martinique when she go dar, and dere I is safe wid a mighty big bankroll in my pocket. It's easy as rollin' off a log.

SMITHERS (*maliciously*). But s'posin' somethin' 'appens wrong an' they do nab yer?

JONES (*decisively*). Dey don't—dat's de answer.

SMITHERS. But, just for argyment's sake—what'd you do?

JONES (*frowning*). I'se got five lead bullets in dis gun good enuff fo' common bush niggers—and after dat I got de silver bullet left to cheat 'em out o' gittin' me.

SMITHERS (*jeeringly*). Ho, I was fergettin' that silver bullet. You'll bump yourself orf in style, won't yer? Blimey!

JONES (*gloomily*). You kin bet yo' whole money on one thing, white man. Dis baby plays out his string to de end and when he quits, he quits wid a bang de way he ought. Silver bullet ain't none too good for him when he go, dat's a fac'! (*Then shaking off his nervousness—with a confident laugh.*) Sho'! What is I talkin' about? Ain't come to dat yit and I never will—not wid trash niggers like dese yere. (*Boastfully.*) Silver bullet bring me luck anyway. I kin outguess, outrun, outfight, an' outplay de whole lot o' dem all ovah de board any time o' de day er night! You watch me!

> (*From the distant hills comes the faint, steady thump of a tom-tom, low and vibrating.*

162

*It starts at a rate exactly corresponding
to normal pulse beat—72 to the minute—
and continues at a gradually accelerating
rate from this point uninterruptedly to
the very end of the play.)*

(*Jones starts at the sound. A strange look of apprehension creeps into his face for a moment as he listens.
Then he asks, with an attempt to regain his most casual
manner*). What's dat drum beatin' fo'?

SMITHERS (*with a mean grin*). For you. That means
the bleedin' ceremony 'as started. I've 'eard it
before and I knows.

JONES. Cer'mony? What cer'mony?

SMITHERS. The blacks is 'oldin' a bloody meetin',
'avin' a war dance, gettin' their courage worked up
b'fore they starts after you.

JONES. Let dem! Dey'll sho' need it!

SMITHERS. And they're there 'oldin' their 'eathen
religious service—makin' no end of devil spells and
charms to 'elp 'em against your silver bullet. (*He
guffaws loudly.*) Blimey, but they're balmy as 'ell!

JONES (*a tiny bit awed and shaken in spite of himself*).
Huh! Takes more'n dat to scare dis chicken!

SMITHERS (*scenting the other's feeling—maliciously*).
Ternight when it's pitch black in the forest, they'll
'ave their pet devils and ghosts 'oundin' after you.
You'll find yer bloody 'air 'll be standin' on end before
termorrow mornin'. (*Seriously.*) It's a bleedin'
queer place, that stinkin' forest, even in daylight.
Yer don't know what might 'appen in there, it's

163

that rotten still. Always sends the cold shivers down my back minute I gets in it.

JONES (*with a contemptuous sniff*). I ain't no white-liver like you is. Trees an' me, we'se friends, and dar's a full moon comin' bring me light. And let dem po' niggers make all de fool spells dey'se a min' to. Does yo' s'pect I'se silly enuff to b'lieve in ghosts an' ha'nts an' all dat ole woman's talk? G'long, white man! You ain't talkin' to me. (*With a chuckle.*) Doesn't you know dey's got to do wid a man who was member in good standin' o' de Baptist Church? Sho' I was dat when I was porter on de Pullmans, befo' I gits into my little trouble. Let dem try deir heathen tricks. De Baptist Church done pertect me and land dem all in hell. (*Then with more confident satisfaction.*) And I'se got little silver bullet o' my own, don't forgit.

SMITHERS. Ho! You 'aven't give much 'eed to your Baptist Church since you been down 'ere. I've 'eard myself you 'ad turned yer coat an' was takin' up with their blarsted witch-doctors, or whatever the 'ell yer calls the swine.

JONES (*vehemently*). I pretends to! Sho' I pretends! Dat's part o' my game from de fust. If I finds out dem niggers believes dat black is white, den I yells it out louder 'n deir loudest. It don't git me nothin' to do missionary work for de Baptist Church. I'se after de coin, an' I lays my Jesus on de shelf for de time bein'. (*Stops abruptly to look at his watch—alertly.*) But I ain't got de time to waste no more fool talk wid you. I'se gwine away

164

from heah dis secon'. (*He reaches in under the throne and pulls out an expensive Panama hat with a bright multi-coloured band and sets it jauntily on his head.*) So long, white man! (*With a grin.*) See you in jail some time, maybe!

SMITHERS. Not me, you won't. Well, I wouldn't be in yer bloody boots for no bloomin' money, but 'ere's wishin' yer luck just the same.

JONES (*contemptuously*). You're de frightenedest man evah I see! I tells you I'se safe's 'f I was in New York City. It takes dem niggers from now to dark to git up de nerve to start somethin'. By dat time, I'se got a head start dey never kotch up wid.

SMITHERS (*maliciously*). Give my regards to any ghosts yer meets up with.

JONES (*grinning*). If dat ghost got money, I'll tell him never ha'nt you less'n he wants to lose it.

SMITHERS (*flattered*). Garn! (*Then curiously.*) Ain't yer takin' no luggage with yer?

JONES. I travels light when I wants to move fast. And I got tinned grub buried on de edge o' de forest. (*Boastfully.*) Now say dat I don't look ahead an' use my brains! (*With a wide, liberal gesture.*) I will all dat's left in de palace to you—and you better grab all you kin sneak away wid befo' dey gits here.

SMITHERS (*gratefully*). Righto—and thanks ter yer. (*As Jones walks towards the door in rear—cautioningly*). Say! Look 'ere, you ain't goin' out that way, are yer?

JONES. Does you think I'd slink out de back door

like a common nigger ? I'se Emperor yit, ain't I ? And de Emperor Jones leaves de way he comes, and dat black trash don't dare stop him—not yit, least-ways. (*He stops for a moment in the doorway, listening to the far-off but insistent beat of the tom-tom.*) Listen to dat roll-call, will you ? Must be mighty big drum carry dat far. (*Then with a laugh.*) Well, if dey ain't no whole brass band to see me off, I sho' got de drum part of it. So long, white man.

> (*He puts his hands in his pockets and with studied carelessness, whistling a tune, he saunters out of the doorway and off to left.*)

SMITHERS (*looks after him with a puzzled admiration*). 'E's got 'is bloomin' nerve with 'im, s'elp me ! (*Then angrily.*) Ho—the bleedin' nigger—puttin' on 'is bloody airs ! I 'opes they nabs 'im an' gives 'im what's what ! (*Then putting business before the pleasure of this thought, looking around him with cupidity.*) A bloke ought to find a 'ole lot in this palace that'd go for a bit of cash. Let's take a look, 'Arry, me lad. (*He starts for the doorway on right as*

THE CURTAIN FALLS

Scene Two: Nightfall

*The end of the plain where the Great Forest begins.
The foreground is sandy, level ground dotted by a
few stones and clumps of stunted bushes cowering
close against the earth to escape the buffeting of
the trade wind. In the rear the forest is a wall
of darkness dividing the world. Only when the
eye becomes accustomed to the gloom can the out-
lines of separate trunks of the nearest trees be
made out, enormous pillars of deeper blackness. A
sombre monotone of wind lost in the leaves moans
in the air. Yet this sound serves but to intensify
the impression of the forest's relentless immobility,
to form a background throwing into relief its brooding,
implacable silence.*

> *(Jones enters from the left, walking rapidly.
> He stops as he nears the edge of the forest,
> looks around him quickly, peering into
> the dark as if searching for some familiar
> landmark. Then, apparently satisfied that
> he is where he ought to be, he throws
> himself on the ground, dog-tired.)*

Well, heah I is. In de nick o' time, too! Little
mo' an' it'd be blacker'n de ace of spades heah-abouts.

(*He pulls a bandana handkerchief from his hip pocket and mops off his perspiring face.*) Sho'! Gimme air! I'se done up sho' 'nuff. Dat soft Emperor job ain't no trainin' for' a long dash ovah dat plain in de brilin' sun. (*Then with a chuckle.*) Cheah up, nigger, de worst is yet to come. (*He lifts his head and stares at the forest. His chuckle peters out abruptly. In a tone of awe.*) My goodness, look at dem woods, will you? Dat no-count Smithers said dey'd be black an' he sho' called de turn. (*Turning away from them quickly and looking down at his feet, he snatches at a chance to change the subject—solicitously.*) Feet, you is holdin' up yo' end fine an' I sutinly hopes you ain't blisterin'. It's time you git a rest. (*He takes off his shoes, his eyes studiously avoiding the forest. He feels the soles of his feet gingerly.*) You is still in de pink—on'y a little mite feverish. Cool yo'selfs. Remember you got a long journey yit before you. (*He sits in a weary attitude, listening to the rhythmic beating of the tom-tom. He grumbles in a loud tone to cover up a growing uneasiness.*) Bush niggers! Wonder dey wouldn' git sick o' beatin' dat drum. Sounds louder, seem like. I wonder if dey's startin' after me? (*He scrambles to his feet, looking back across the plain.*) Couldn't see dem now, nohow, if dey was hundred feet away. (*Then shaking himself like a wet dog to get rid of these depressing thoughts.*) Sho', dey's miles an' miles behind. What you gittin' fidgety about? (*But he sits down and begins to lace up his shoes in great haste, all the time muttering reassuringly.*) You know what? Yo' belly is empty, dat's what's de matter wid you. Come time to eat!

168

Wid nothin' but wind on yo' stumach, o' course you feels jiggedy. Well, we eats right heah an' now soon's I gits dese here shoes laced up. (*He finishes lacing up his shoes.*) Dere! Now le's see! (*Gets on his hands and knees and searches the ground around him with his eyes.*) White stone, white stone, where is you? (*He sees the first white stone and crawls to it—with satisfaction.*) Heah you is! I knowed dis was de right place. Box of grub, come to me. (*He turns over the stone and feels in under it—in a tone of dismay.*) Ain't heah! Gorry, is I in de right place or isn't I? Dere's 'nother stone. Guess dat's it. (*He scrambles to the next stone and turns it over.*) Ain't heah, neither! Grub, whar is you? Ain't heah. Gorry, has I got to go hungry into dem woods—all de night? (*While he is talking he scrambles from one stone to another, turning them over in frantic haste. Finally he jumps to his feet excitedly.*) Is I lost de place? Must have! But how dat happen when I was followin' de trail across de plain in broad daylight? (*Almost plaintively.*) I'se hungry, I is! I gotta git my feed. Whar's my strength gonna come from if I doesn't? Gorry, I gotta find dat grub high an' low somehow! Why it come dark so quick like dat? Can't see nothin'. (*He scratches a match on his trousers and peers about him. The rate of the beat of the far-off tom-tom increases perceptibly as he does so. He mutters in a bewildered voice.*) How come all dese white stones come heah when I only remembers one? (*Suddenly, with a frightened gasp, he flings the match on the ground and stamps on it.*) Nigger, is you gone crazy mad? Is you lightin' matches

169

to show dem whar you is? Fo' Lawd's sake, use yo' haid. Gorry, I'se got to be careful! (*He stares at the plain behind him apprehensively, his hand on his revolver.*) But how come all dese white stones? And whar's dat tin box o' grub I hid all wrapped up in oil cloth?

> (*While his back is turned, the Little Formless Fears creep out from the deeper blackness of the forest. They are black, shapeless, only their glittering little eyes can be seen. If they have any describable form at all it is that of a grubworm about the size of a creeping child. They move noiselessly, but with deliberate, painful effort, striving to raise themselves on end, failing and sinking prone again. Jones turns about to face the forest. He stares up at the tops of the trees, seeking vainly to discover his whereabouts by their conformation.*)

Can't tell nothin' from dem trees! Gorry, nothin' 'round heah look like I evah seed it befo'. I'se gone lost de place sho' 'nuff. (*With mournful foreboding.*) It's mighty queer! It's mighty queer! (*With sudden forced defiance—in an angry tone.*) Woods, is you tryin' to put somethin' ovah on me?

(*From the formless creatures on the ground in front of him comes a tiny gale of low mocking laughter like a rustling of leaves. They squirm upward towards him in twisted attitudes. Jones looks down, leaps backwards with a yell of terror, pulling out his revolver as he does so—in a quavering voice.*) What's dat. Who's

dar? What is you? Git away from me befo' I
shoots! You don't?——

> (*He fires. There is a flash, a loud report, then
> silence broken only by the far-off quickened
> throb of the tom-tom. The formless
> creatures have scurried back into the
> forest. Jones remains fixed in his position
> listening intently. The sound of the
> shot, the reassuring feel of the revolver in
> his hand, have somewhat restored his
> shaken nerve. He addresses himself with
> renewed confidence.*)

Dey're gone. Dat shot fix 'em. Dey was only
little animals—little wild pigs, I reckon. Dey've
maybe rooted out yo' grub an' eat it. Sho', you
fool nigger, what you think dey is—ha'nts. (*Excitedly.*)
Gorry, you give de game away when you fire dat
shot. Dem niggers heah dat fo' su'tin! Time you
beat it in de woods widout no long waits. (*He starts
for the forest—hesitates before the plunge—then urging
himself in with manful resolution.*) Git in, nigger!
What you skeered at? Ain't nothin' dere but de
trees! Git in! (*He plunges boldly into the forest.*)

Scene Three

Nine o'clock. In the forest. The moon has just risen. Its beams, drifting through the canopy of leaves, make a barely perceptible, suffused, eerie glow. A dense low wall of underbrush and creepers is in the nearer foreground, fencing in a small triangular clearing. Beyond this is the massed blackness of the forest like an encompassing barrier. A path is dimly discerned leading down to the clearing from left, rear, and winding away from it again towards the right. As the scene opens nothing can be distinctly made out. Except for the beating of the tom-tom, which is a trifle louder and quicker than in the previous scene, there is silence, broken every few seconds by a queer, clicking sound. Then gradually the figure of the negro, Jeff, can be discerned crouching on his haunches at the rear of the triangle. He is middle-aged, thin, brown in colour, is dressed in a Pullman porter's uniform, cap, etc. He is throwing a pair of dice on the ground before him, picking them up, shaking them, casting them out with the regular, rigid, mechanical movements of an automaton. The heavy, plodding footsteps of someone approaching along the trail from the left are heard and Jones'

*voice, pitched in a slightly higher key and strained
in a cheering effort to overcome its own tremors.*

De moon's rizen.   Does you heah dat, nigger ?   You
gits more light from dis forrard.   No mo' buttin' yo'
fool head agin' de trunks an' scratchin' de hide off
yo' legs in de bushes.   Now you sees whar you'se
gwine.   So cheer up !   From now on you has it easy.
(*He steps just to the rear of the triangular clearing
and mops off his face on his sleeve.   He has lost his
Panama hat.   His face is scratched, his brilliant uniform
shows several large rents.*)   What time's it gittin' to
be, I wonder ?   I dassent light no match to find out.
Phoo'.   It's wa'm an' dats a fac' !   (*Wearily.*)   How
long I been makin' trampin' dese woods ?   Must be
hours an' hours.   Seems like fo'evah !   Yit can't be,
when de moon's jes' riz.   Dis am a long night fo'
yo', yo' Majesty !   (*With a mournful chuckle.*)   Majesty !
Der ain't much majesty 'bout dis baby now.
(*With attempted cheerfulness.*)   Never min'.   It's
all part o' de game.   Dis night come to an end
like everything else.   And when you gits dar safe
and has dat bankroll in yo' hands you laughs at all
dis.   (*He starts to whistle, but checks himself abruptly.*)
What yo' whistlin' for, you po' fool !   Want all de
worl' to heah you ?   (*He stops talking to listen.*)
Heah dat ole drum !   Sho' gits nearer from de sound.
Dey're takin' it along wid 'em.   Time fo' me to
move.   (*He takes a step forward, then stops—worriedly.*)
What's dat odder queer clicketty sound I heah ?   Dere
it is !   Sound close !   Sound like—sound like—Fo' God
sake, sound like some nigger was shootin' dice !
(*Frightenedly.*)   I better get on quick when I gits

173

dem notions. (*He walks quickly into the clear space —then stands transfixed as he sees Jeff—in a terrified gasp.*) Who dar ? Who dat ? Is dat you, Jeff ? (*Starting towards the other, forgetful for a moment of his surroundings and really believing it is a living man that he sees—in a tone of happy relief.*) Jeff ! I'se sho' mighty glad to see you ! Dey tols me you done died from dat razor cut I give' you. (*Stopping suddenly, bewildered*). But how you come to be heah, nigger ? (*He stares fascinatedly at the other who continues his mechanical play with the dice. Jones' eyes began to roll wildly. He stutters.*) Ain't you gwine—look up—can't you speak to me ? Is you—is you—a ha'nt ? (*He jerks out his revolver in a frenzy of terrified rage.*) Nigger, I kills you dead once. Has I got to kill you agin ? You take it den. (*He fires. When the smoke clears away Jeff has disappeared. Jones stands trembling—then with a certain reassurance.*) He's gone, anyway. Ha'nt or no ha'nt, dat shot fix him. (*The beat of the far-off tom-tom is perceptibly louder and more rapid. Jones becomes conscious of it—with a start, looking back over his shoulder.*) Dey's gittin' near ! Dey'se comin' fast ! And heah I is shootin' shots to let 'em know jes' whar I is. Oh, Gorry, I'se got to run. (*Forgetting the path he plunges wildly into the underbrush in the rear and disappears in the shadow.*)

Scene Four

*Eleven o'clock. In the forest. A wide dirt road runs
diagonally from right, front, to left, rear. Rising
sheer on both sides the forest walls it in. The moon
is now up. Under its light the road glimmers
ghastly and unreal. It is as if the forest has
stood aside momentarily to let the road pass through
and accomplish its veiled purpose. This done, the
forest will fold in upon itself again and the road
will be no more. Jones stumbles in from the forest
on the right. His uniform is ragged and torn.
He looks about him with numbed surprise when
he sees the road, his eyes blinking in the bright
moonlight. He flops down exhaustedly and pants
heavily for a while. Then with sudden anger.*

I'm meltin' wid heat! Runnin' an' runnin' an'
runnin'! Damn dis heah coat! Like a strait jacket!
(*He tears off his coat and flings it away from him,
revealing himself stripped to the waist.*) Dere! Dat's
better! ⟩Now I kin breathe! (*Looking down at
his feet, the spurs catch his eye.*) And to hell wid dese
high-fangled spurs. Dey're what's been a-trippin' me
up an' breakin' me neck. (*He unstraps them and*

175

flings them away disgustedly.) Dere! I gits rid o'
dem frippety Emperor trappin's an' I travels lighter.
Lawd! I'se tired! (*After a pause, listening to the
insistent beat of the tom-tom in the distance*.) I must
'a put some distance between myself an' dem—runnin'
like dat—and yit—dat damn drum sound jes' de
same—nearer, even. Well, I guess I a'most holds
my lead anyhow. Dey won't nevei catch up. (*With
a sigh*.) If on'y my fool legs stands up. Oh, I'se
sorry I evah went in for dis. Dat Emperor job is
sho' hard to shake. (*He looks around him suspiciously*.)
How'd dis road evah git heah? Good level road,
too. I never remembers seein' if befo'. (*Shaking his
head apprehensively*.) Dese woods is sho' full o' de
queerest things at night. (*With a sudden terror*.)
Lawd God, don't let me see no more o' dem ha'nts!
Dey gits me scared! (*Then trying to talk himself into
confidence*.) Ha'nts! You fool nigger, dey ain't no
such things! Don't de Baptist parson tell you dat
many time? Is you civilised, or is you like dese
ign'rent black niggers heah? Sho'! Dat was all
in yo' own head. Wasn't nothin' dere. Wasn't
no Jeff! Know what? You jus' get seein' dem
things 'cause yo' belly's empty and you's sick wid
hunger inside. Hunger 'fects yo' head and yo' eyes.
Any fool know dat. (*Then pleading fervently*.) But
bless God, I don't come across no more o' dem, whatever dey is! (*Then cautiously*.) Rest! Don't talk!
Rest! You needs it. Den you gits on yo' way again.
(*Looking at the moon*.) Night's half gone a'most. You
hits de coast in de mawning! Den you'se all safe.

(*From the right forward a small gang of*

negroes enter. They are dressed in striped convict suits, their heads are shaven, one leg drags limpingly, shackled to a heavy ball and chain. Some carry picks, the others shovels. They are followed by a white man dressed in the uniform of a prison guard. A Winchester rifle is slung across his shoulders and he carries a heavy whip. At a signal from the guard they stop on the road opposite where Jones is sitting. Jones, who has been staring up at the sky, unmindful of their noiseless approach, suddenly looks down and sees them. His eyes pop out, he tries to get to his feet and fly, but sinks back, too numbed by fright to move. His voice catches in a choking prayer.)

Lawd Jesus !

(The prison guard cracks his whip—noiselessly —and at that signal all the convicts start at work on the road. They swing their picks, they shovel, but not a sound comes from their labour. Their movements, like those of Jeff in the preceding scene, are those of automatons—rigid, slow, and mechanical. The prison guard points sternly at Jones with his whip, motions him to take his place among the other shovellers. Jones gets to his feet in a hypnotised stupor. He mumbles subserviently.)

177

Yes, suh! Yes, suh! I'se comin'.

> (*As he shuffles, dragging one foot, over to his place, he curses under his breath with rage and hatred.*)

God damn yo' soul, I gits even wid you yit, some time.

> (*As if there were a shovel in his hands he goes through weary, mechanical gestures of digging up dirt, and throwing it to the roadside. Suddenly the guard approaches him angrily, threateningly. He raises his whip and lashes Jones viciously across the shoulders with it. Jones winces with pain and cowers abjectly. The guard turns his back on him and walks away contemptuously. Instantly Jones straightens up. With arms upraised as if his shovel were a club in his hands he springs murderously at the unsuspecting guard. In the act of crashing down his shovel on the white man's skull, Jones suddenly becomes aware that his hands are empty. He cries despairingly.*)

Whar's my shovel? Gimme my shovel 'till I splits his damn head! (*Appealing to his fellow convicts.*) Gimme a shovel, one o' you, fo' God's sake!

> (*They stand fixed in motionless attitudes, their eyes on the ground. The guard seems to wait expectantly, his back turned to the attacker. Jones bellows with baffled, terrified rage, tugging frantically at his revolver.*)

I kills you, you white debil, if it's de last thing I
evah does! Ghost or debil, I kill you agin!

> (*He frees the revolver and fires point blank at
> the guard's back. Instantly the walls of
> the forest close in from both sides, the
> road and the figures of the convict gang
> are blotted out in an enshrouding darkness.
> The only sounds are a crashing in the
> underbrush as Jones leaps away in mad
> flight and the throbbing of the tom-tom,
> still far distant, but increased in volume
> of sound and rapidity of beat.*)

Scene Five

*One o'clock. A large circular clearing, enclosed by the
serried ranks of gigantic trunks of tall trees whose
tops are lost to view. In the centre is a big dead
stump worn by time into a curious resemblance to
an auction block. The moon floods the clearing
with a clear light. Jones forces his way in through
the forest on the left. He looks wildly about the
clearing with hunted, fearful glances. His trousers
are in tatters, his shoes cut and misshapen, flapping
about his feet. He slinks cautiously to the stump in the
centre and sits down in a tense position, ready for
instant flight. Then he holds his head in his hands and
rocks back and forth, moaning to himself miserably.)*

Oh Lawd, Lawd! Oh Lawd, Lawd! *(Suddenly
he throws himself on his knees and raises his clasped
hands to the sky—in a voice of agonised pleading.)*
Lawd Jesus, heah my prayer! I'se a po' sinner, a
po' sinner! I knows I done wrong, I knows it!
When I cotches Jeff cheatin' wid loaded dice my
anger overcomes me and I kills him dead! Lawd,
I done wrong! When dat guard hits me wid de
whip, my anger overcomes me, and I kills him dead.
Lawd, I done wrong! And down heah whar dese

180

fool bush niggers raises me up to the seat o' de mighty,
I steals all I could grab. Lawd, I done wrong! I
knows it! I'se sorry! Forgive me, Lawd! Forgive
dis po' sinner! (*Then beseeching terrifiedly.*) And keep
dem away, Lawd! Keep dem away from me! And
stop dat drum soundin' in my ears! Dat begin to
sound ha'nted, too. (*He gets to his feet, evidently
slightly reassured by his prayer—with attempted confidence.*) De Lawd'll preserve me from dem ha'nts
after dis. (*Sits down on the stump again.*) I ain't
skeered o' real men. Let dem come. But dem
odders—— (*He shudders—then looks down at his
feet, working his toes inside the shoes—with a groan.*)
Oh, my po' feet! Dem shoes ain't no use no more
'ceptin' to hurt. I'se better off widout dem. (*He
unlaces them and pulls them off—holds the wrecks of
the shoes in his hands and regards them mournfully.*) You
was real, A-one patin' leather, too. Look at you now.
Emperor, you'se gittin' mighty low!

> (*He sighs dejectedly and remains with bowed
> shoulders, staring down at the shoes in his
> hands as if reluctant to throw them away.
> While his attention is thus occupied, a
> crowd of figures silently enter the clearing
> from all sides. All are dressed in
> Southern costumes of the period of the
> fifties of the last century. There are
> middle-aged men who are evidently well-
> to-do planters. There is one spruce,
> authoritative individual—the Auctioneer.
> There are a crowd of curious spectators,
> chiefly young belles and dandies who have*

come to the slave-market for diversion. All exchange courtly greetings in dumb show and chat silently together. There is something stiff, rigid, unreal, marionettish about their movements. They group themselves about the stump. Finally a batch of slaves are led in from the left by an attendant—three men of different ages, two women, one with a baby in her arms, nursing. They are placed to the left of the stump, beside Jones.

The white planters look them over appraisingly as if they were cattle. The dandies point their fingers and make witty remarks. The belles titter bewitchingly. All this in silence save for the ominous throb of the tom-tom. The Auctioneer holds up his hand, taking his place at the stump. The groups strain forward. He touches Jones on the shoulder peremptorily, motioning for him to stand on the stump—the auction block.

Jones looks up, sees the figures on all sides, looks wildly for some opening to escape, sees none, screams and leaps madly to the top of the stump to get as far away from them as possible. He stands there, cowering, paralysed with horror. The Auctioneer begins his silent speech. · He points to Jones, appeals to the planters to see for themselves. Here is a good field hand, sound in wind and limb as they can see. Very strong still in spite

*of his being middle-aged. Look at that
back. Look at those shoulders. Look at
the muscles in his arms and his sturdy
legs. Capable of any amount of hard
labour. Moreover of a good disposition,
intelligent and tractable. Will any
gentleman start the bidding? The
planters raise their fingers, make their
bids. They are apparently all eager to
possess Jones. The bidding is lively, the
crowd interested. While this has been
going on, Jones has been seized by the
courage of desperation. He dares to look
down and around him. Over his face
abject terror gives way to mystification,
to gradual realisation—stutteringly.)*

What you all doin', white folks? What's all dis?
What you all lookin' at me fo'? What you doin'
wid me, anyhow? *(Suddenly convulsed with raging
hatred and fear.)* Is dis a auction? Is you sellin'
me like dey uster befo' de war? *(Jerking out his
revolver just as the Auctioneer knocks him down to
one of the planters—glaring from him to the purchaser.)*
And *you* sells me? And *you* buys me? I shows **you**
I'se a free nigger, damn yo' souls!

> *(He fires at the Auctioneer and at the planter
> with such rapidity that the two shots are al-
> most simultaneous. As if this were a signal
> the walls of the forest fold in. Only blackness
> remains and silence broken by Jones as he
> rushes off, crying with fear—and by the
> quickened, ever louder beat of the tom-tom.)*

183

Scene Six

Three o'clock. A cleared space in the forest. The limbs of the trees meet over it forming a low ceiling about five feet from the ground. The interlocked ropes of creepers reaching upward to entwine the tree trunks gives an arched appearance to the sides. The space thus enclosed is like the dark, noisome hold of some ancient vessel. The moonlight is almost completely shut out and only a vague, wan light filters through. There is the noise of someone approaching from the left, stumbling and crawling through the undergrowth. Jones' voice is heard between chattering moans.

Oh, Lawd, what I gwine do now? Ain't got no bullet left on'y de silver one. If mo' o' dem ha'nts come after me, how I gwine skeer dem away? Oh, Lawd, on'y de silver one left—an' I gotta save dat fo' luck. If I shoots dat one I'm a goner sho'! Lawd, it's black heah! Whar's de moon? Oh, Lawd, don't dis night evah come to an end? *(By the sounds, he is feeling his way cautiously forward.)* Dere! Dis feels like a clear space. I gotta lie down an' rest. I don't care if dem niggers does cotch me. I gotta rest.

(He is well forward now where his figure can
be dimly made out. His trousers have been
so torn away that what is left of them is no
better than a loin cloth. He flings himself full length, face downward on the
ground, panting with exhaustion. Gradually it seems to grow lighter in the enclosed
space and two rows of seated figures can
be seen behind Jones. They are sitting
in crumpled, despairing attitudes,
hunched, facing one another with their
backs touching the forest walls as if they
were shackled to them. All are negroes
naked save for loin cloths. At first
they are silent and motionless. Then
they begin to sway slowly forward towards
each and back again in unison, as if
they were laxly letting themselves follow
the long roll of a ship at sea. At the
same time a low, melancholy murmur
rises among them, increasing gradually
by rhythmic degrees which seem to be
directed and controlled by the throb of
the tom-tom in the distance, to a long,
tremulous wail of despair that reaches a
certain pitch, unbearably acute, then
falls by slow gradations of tone into
silence and is taken up again. Jones
starts, looks up, sees the figures, and throws
himself down again to shut out the sight.
A shudder of terror shakes his whole body
as the wail rises up about him again..

But the next time his voice, as if under some uncanny compulsion, starts with the others. As their chorus lifts he rises to a sitting posture similar to the others, swaying back and forth. His voice reaches the highest pitch of sorrow, of desolation. The light fades out, the other voices cease, and only darkness is left. Jones can be heard scrambling to his feet and running off, his voice sinking down the scale and receding as he moves farther and farther away in the forest. The tom-tom beats louder, quicker, with a more insistent, triumphant pulsation.)

Scene Seven

*Five o'clock.   The foot of a gigantic tree by the edge
of a great river. A rough structure of boulders,
like an altar, is by the tree. The raised river
bank is in the nearer background. Beyond this the
surface of the river spreads out, brilliant and un-
ruffled in the moonlight, blotted out and merged
into a veil of bluish mist in the distance. Jones'
voice is heard from the left rising and falling in
the long, despairing wail of the chained slaves, to
the rhythmic beat of the tom-tom. As his voice
sinks into silence, he enters the open space. The
expression of his face is fixed and stony, his eyes
have an obsessed glare, he moves with a strange
deliberation like a sleep-walker or one in a trance.
He looks around at the tree, the rough stone altar,
the moonlit surface of the river beyond, and passes
his hand over his head with a vague gesture of
puzzled bewilderment. Then, as if in obedience
to some obscure impulse, he sinks into a kneeling,
devotional posture before the altar. Then he seems
to come to himself partly, to have an uncertain realisation of what he is doing, for he straightens up and
stares about him horrifiedly—in an incoherent mumble.*

What—what is I doin'? What is—dis place? Seems like—seems like I know dat tree—an' dem stones—an' de river. I remember—seems like I been heah befo'. (*Tremblingly.*) Oh, Gorry, I'se skeered in dis place! I'se skeered! Oh, Lawd, pertect dis sinner!

> (*Crawling away from the altar, he cowers close to the ground, his face hidden, his shoulders heaving with sobs of hysterical fright. From behind the trunk of the tree, as if he had sprung out of it, the figure of the Congo Witch-Doctor appears. He is wizened and old, naked except for the fur of some small animal tied about his waist, its bushy tail hanging down in front. His body is stained all over a bright red. Antelope horns are on each side of his head, branching upward. In one hand he carries a bone rattle, in the other a charm stick with a bunch of white cockatoo feathers tied to the end. A great number of glass beads and bone ornaments are about his neck, ears, wrists, and ankles. He struts noiselessly with a queer prancing step to a position in the clear ground between Jones and the altar. Then with a preliminary, *summoning stamp of his foot on the earth, he begins to dance and to chant. As if in response to his summons the beating of the tom-tom grows to a fierce, exultant boom whose throbs seem to fill the air with vibrating rhythm.*

Jones looks up, starts to spring to his feet, reaches a half-kneeling, half-squatting position and remains rigidly fixed there, paralysed with awed fascination by this new apparition. The Witch-Doctor sways, stamping with his foot, his bone rattle clicking the time. His voice rises and falls in a weird, monotonous croon, without articulate word divisions. Gradually his dance becomes clearly one of a narrative in pantomime, his croon is an incantation, a charm to allay the fierceness of some implacable deity demanding sacrifice. He flees, he is pursued by devils, he hides, he flees again. Ever wilder and wilder becomes his flight, nearer and nearer draws the pursuing evil, more and more the spirit of terror gains possession of him. His croon, rising to intensity, is punctuated by shrill cries. Jones has become completely hypnotised. His voice joins in the incantation, in the cries, he beats time with his hands and sways his body to and fro from the waist. The whole spirit and meaning of the dance has entered into him, has become his spirit. Finally the theme of the pantomime halts on a howl of despair, and is taken up again in a note of savage hope. There is a salvation. The forces of evil demand sacrifice. They must be appeased. The

189

*Witch-Doctor points with his wand to
the sacred tree, to the river beyond, to
the altar, and finally to Jones with a
ferocious command. Jones seems to sense
the meaning of this. It is he who must
offer himself for sacrifice. He beats his
forehead abjectly to the ground, moaning
hysterically.)*

Mercy, oh Lawd! Mercy! Mercy on dis po' sinner.

*(The Witch-Doctor springs to the river bank.
He stretches out his arms and calls to
some god within its depths. Then he
starts backward slowly, his arms remaining
out. A huge head of a crocodile appears
over the bank and its eyes, glittering
greenly, fasten upon Jones. He stares into
them fascinatedly. The Witch-Doctor
prances up to him, touches him with his
wand, motions with hideous command
towards the waiting monster. Jones
squirms on his belly nearer and nearer,
moaning continually.)*

Mercy, Lawd! Mercy!

*(The crocodile heaves more of his enormous
hulk on to the land. Jones squirms towards him. The Witch-Doctor's voice
shrills out in furious exultation, the
tom-tom beats madly. Jones cries out in
a fierce, exhausted spasm of anguished
pleading.)*

Lawd, save me! Lawd Jesus, heah my prayer!

(Immediately, in answer to his prayer, comes the thought of the one bullet left him. He snatches at his hip, shouting defiantly.)

De silver bullet! You don't git me yit!

(He fires at the green eyes in front of him. The head of the crocodile sinks back behind the river bank, the Witch-Doctor springs behind the sacred tree and disappears. Jones lies with his face to the ground, his arms outstretched, whimpering with fear as the throb of the tom-tom fills the silence about him with a sombre pulsation, a baffled but revengeful power.)

Scene Eight

Dawn. Same as Scene Two, the dividing line of forest and plain. The nearest tree trunks are dimly revealed, but the forest behind them is still a mass of glooming shadow. The tom-tom seems on the very spot, so loud and continuously vibrating are its beats. Lem enters from the left, followed by a small squad of his soldiers, and by the Cockney trader, Smithers. Lem is a heavy-set, ape-faced old savage of the extreme African type, dressed only in a loin cloth. A revolver and cartridge belt are about his waist. His soldiers are in different degrees of rag-concealed nakedness. All wear broad palm-leaf hats. Each one carries a rifle. Smithers is the same as in Scene One. One of the soldiers, evidently a tracker, is peering about keenly on the ground. He grunts and points to the spot where Jones entered the forest. Lem and Smithers come to look.

SMITHERS (*after a glance, turns away in disgust*). That's where 'e went in right enough. Much good it'll do yer. 'E's miles orf by this an' safe to the coast, damn 's 'ide! I tole yer yer'd lose 'im, didn't I ?—wastin' the 'ole bloomin' night beatin' yer

bloody drum and castin' yer silly spells! Gawd
blimey, wot a pack!

LEM (*gutturally*). We cotch him. You see. (*He
makes a motion to his soldiers who squat down on their
haunches in a semi-circle.*)

SMITHERS (*exasperatedly*). Well, ain't yer goin' in
an' 'unt 'im in the woods? What the 'ell's the good
of waitin'?

LEM (*imperturbably—squatting down himself*). We
cotch him.

SMITHERS (*turning away from him contemptuously*).
Aw! Garn! 'E's a better man than the lot o'
you put together. I 'ates the sight o' 'im, but I'll
say that for 'im.

> (*A sound of snapping twigs comes from the
> forest. The soldiers jump to their feet,
> cocking their rifles alertly. Lem
> remains sitting with an imperturbable
> expression, but listening intently. The
> sound from the woods is repeated. Lem
> makes a quick signal with his hand. His
> followers creep quickly but noiselessly
> into the forest, scattering so that each
> enters at a different spot.*)

SMITHERS (*in the silence that follows—in a contemptuous whisper*). You ain't thinkin' that would be 'im, I
'ope?

LEM (*calmly*). We cotch him.

SMITHERS. Blarsted fat 'eads! (*Then after a
second's thought—wonderingly*). Still, after all, it might
'appen. If 'e lost 'is bloody way in these stinkin'

woods 'e'd likely turn in a circle without 'is knowin' it. They all does.

LEM (*peremptorily*). Ssshh! (*The reports of several rifles sound from the forest, followed a second later by savage, exultant yells. The beating of the tom-tom abruptly ceases. Lem looks up at the white man with a grin of satisfaction.*) We cotch him. Him dead.

SMITHERS (*with a snarl*). 'Ow d'yer know it's 'im, an' 'ow d'yer know 'e's dead?

LEM. My mens dey got 'um silver bullets. Dey kill him shure.

SMITHERS (*astonished*). They got silver bullets?

LEM. Lead bullet no kill him. He got um strong charm. I cook um money, make um silver bullet, make um strong charm, too.

SMITHERS (*light breaking upon him*). So that's wot you was up to all night, wot? You was scared to put after 'im till you'd moulded silver bullets, eh?

LEM (*simply stating a fact*). Yes. Him got strong charm. Lead no good.

SMITHERS (*slapping his thigh and guffawing*). Haw-haw! If yer don't beat all 'ell! (*Then recovering himself—scornfully.*) I'll bet yer it ain't 'im they shot at all, yer bleedin' looney!

LEM (*calmly*). Dey come bring him now. (*The soldiers come out of the forest, carrying Jones's limp body. There is a little reddish-purple hole under his left breast. He is dead. They carry him to Lem, who examines his body with great satisfaction. Smithers leans over his shoulder—in a tone of frightened awe.*) Well, they

194

did for yer right enough, Jonesy, me lad! Dead as a bloater! (*Mockingly.*) Where's yer 'igh an' mighty airs now, yer bloomin' Majesty? (*Then with a grin.*) Silver bullets! Gawd blimey, but yer died in the 'eighth o' style, any'ow! (*Lem makes a motion to the soldiers to carry the body out, left. Smithers speaks to him sneeringly.*)

SMITHERS. And I s'pose you think it's yer bleedin' charms and yer silly beatin' the drum that made 'im run in a circle when 'e'd lost 'imself, don't yer? (*But Lem makes no reply, does not seem to hear the question, walks out, left, after his men. Smithers looks after him with contemptuous scorn.*) Stupid as 'ogs, the lot of 'em! Blarsted niggers!

THE CURTAIN FALLS

Diff'rent

Diff'rent
Act One

Characters

CAPTAIN CALEB WILLIAMS

EMMA CROSBY

CAPTAIN JOHN CROSBY, *her father*

MRS. CROSBY, *her mother*

JACK CROSBY, *her brother*

HARRIET WILLIAMS, *Caleb's sister (later Mrs. Rogers)*

ALFRED ROGERS

BENNY ROGERS, *their son*

Act One

Parlour of the Crosby home on a side street of a seaport village in New England—mid-afternoon of a day in late spring in the year 1890.

Act Two

The same. Late afternoon of a day in the early spring of the year 1920.

Act One

Parlour of the Crosby home. The room is small and low-ceilinged. Everything has an aspect of scrupulous neatness. On the left, forward, a stiff plush-covered chair. Farther back, in order, a window looking out on a vegetable garden, a black horsehair sofa, and another window. In the far left corner, an old mahogany chest of drawers. To the right of it, in rear, a window looking out on the front garden. To the right of this window is the front door, reached by a gravel path through the small lawn which separates the house from the street. To the right of door, another window. In the far right corner, a diminutive, old-fashioned piano with a stool in front of it. Near the piano on the right, a door leading to the next room. On this side of the room are also a small book-case half filled with old volumes, a big open fireplace, and another plush-covered chair. Over the fireplace a mantelpiece with marble clock and figure groups either side. The walls are papered a brown colour. The floor is covered with a dark carpet. In the centre of the room there is a clumsy, marble-topped table. On the table a large china lamp, a bulky Bible with a brass clasp, and books that look like cheap novels. Near the table, three plush covered chairs, two of which are rockers. Several enlarged photos of uncomfortable stern-looking people are hung on the walls.

It is mid-afternoon of a fine day in late spring of the year 1890. Bright sunlight streams through the windows on the left. Through the window and the screen door in the rear the fresh green of the lawn and of the elm trees that line the street can be seen. Stiff white curtains are at all the windows.

As the curtain rises Emma Crosby and Caleb Williams are discovered. Emma is a slender girl of twenty, rather under medium height. Her face, in spite of plain features, gives an impression of prettiness, due to large, soft blue eyes which have an incongruous quality of romantic dreaminess about them. Her mouth and chin are heavy, full of a self-willed stubbornness. Although her body is slight, there is a quick, nervous vitality about her movements that reveals an underlying constitution of reserve power and health. She has light brown hair, thick and heavy. She is dressed soberly and neatly in her black Sunday best style of the period.

Caleb Williams is tall and powerfully built, about thirty. Black hair, keen dark eyes, face rugged and bronzed, mouth obstinate but good-natured. He also is got up in black Sunday best and is uncomfortably self-conscious and stiff therein.

They are sitting on the horsehair sofa, side by side. His arm is about her waist. She holds one of his big hands in both of hers, her head leaning back against his shoulder, her eyes half closed in a dreamy contentedness. He stares before him rigidly, his whole attitude wooden and fixed as if he were posing for a photograph ; yet his eyes are expressively tender and protecting when he glances down at her diffidently out of the corners without moving his head.

EMMA (*sighing happily*). Gosh, I wish we could sit this way for ever ! (*Then after a pause, as he makes no comment except a concurring squeeze.*) Don't you, Caleb ?

CALEB (*with another squeeze—emphatically*). Hell, yes ! I'd like it, Emmer.

EMMA (*softly*). I do wish you wouldn't swear so awful much, Caleb.

CALEB. S'cuse me, Emmer, it jumped out o' my mouth afore I thought. (*Then with a grin.*) You'd ought to be used to that part o' men's wickedness—with your Pa and Jack cussin' about the house all the time.

EMMA (*with a smile*). Oh, I haven't no strict religious notions about it. I'm hardened in sin so far's they're concerned. Goodness me, how would Ma and me ever have lived in the same house with them two if we wasn't used to it ? I don't even notice their cussing no more. And I don't mind hearing it from the other men, either. Being sea-faring men, away from their women folks most of the time, I know it just gets to be part of their natures and they ain't responsible. (*Decisively.*) But you're diff'rent. You just got to be diff'rent from the rest.

CALEB (*amused by her seriousness*). Diff'rent ? Ain't I a sea-farin' man, too ?

205

EMMA. You're diff'rent just the same. That's what made me fall in love with you 'stead of any of them. And you've got to stay di'ffrent. Promise me, Caleb, that you'll always stay diff'rent from them—even after we're married years and years.

CALEB (*embarrassed*). Why—I promise to do my best by you, Emmer. You know that, don't ye? On'y don't git the notion in your head I'm any better'n the rest. They're all good men—most of 'em, anyway. Don't tell me, for instance, you think I'm better'n your Pa or Jack—'cause I ain't. And I don't know as I'd want to be, neither.

EMMA (*excitedly*). But you got to want to be—when I ask it.

CALEB (*surprised*). Better'n your Pa?

EMMA (*struggling to convey her meaning*). Why, Pa's all right. He's a fine man—and Jack's all right, too. I wouldn't hear a bad word about them for anything. And the others are all right in their way, too, I s'pose. Only—don't you see what I mean?—I look on you as diff'rent from all of them. I mean there's things that's all right for them to do that wouldn't be for you—in my mind, anyway.

CALEB (*puzzled and a bit uneasy*). Sailors ain't plaster saints, Emmer—not a darn one of 'em ain't!

EMMA (*hurt and disappointed*). Then you won't promise me to stay diff'rent for my sake?

CALEB (*with rough tenderness*). Oh, hell, Emmer, I'll do any cussed thing in the world you want me to, and you know it!

206

EMMA (*lovingly*). Thank you, Caleb. It means a lot to me—more'n you think. And don't you think I'm diff'rent, too—not just the same as all the other girls hereabouts?

CALEB 'Course you be! Ain't I always said that? You're wo'th the whole pack of 'em put together.

EMMA. Oh, I don't mean I'm any better. I mean I just look at things diff'rent from what they do— getting married, for example, and other things, too. And so I've got it fixed in my head that you and me ought to make a married couple—diff'rent from the rest—not that they ain't all right in their way.

CALEB (*puzzled—uncertainly*). Waal—it's bound to be from your end of it, you bein' like you are. But I ain't so sure o' mine.

EMMA. Well, I am!

CALEB (*with a grin*). You got me scared, Emmer. I'm scared you'll want me to live up to one of them high-fangled heroes you been readin' about in them books. (*He indicates the novels on the table.*)

EMMA. No, I don't. I want you to be just like yourself, that's all.

CALEB. That's easy. It ain't hard bein' a plain, ordinary cuss.

EMMA. You are not!

CALEB (*with a laugh*). Remember, I'm warnin' you, Emmer; and after we're married and you find me out, you can't say I got you under no false pretences.

EMMA (*laughing*). I won't. I won't ever need to. (*Then after a pause.*) Just think, it's only two days more before you and me'll be man and wife.

CALEB (*squeezing her*). Waal, it's about time, ain't it?—after waitin' three years for me to git enough money saved—and us not seein' hide or hair of each other the last two of 'em. (*With a laugh.*) Shows ye what trust I put in you, Emmer, when I kin go off on a two year whalin' vige and leave you all 'lone for all the young fellers in town to make eyes at.

EMMA. But lots and lots of the others does the same thing without thinking nothing about it.

CALEB (*with a laugh*). Yes, but I'm diff'rent, like you says.

EMMA (*laughing*). Oh, you're poking fun now.

CALEB (*with a wink*). And you know as well's me that some o' the others finds out some funny things that's been done when they was away.

EMMA (*laughing at first*). Yes, but you know I'm diff'rent, too. (*Then frowning.*) But don't let's talk about that sort o' ructions. I hate to think of such things—even joking. I ain't like that sort.

CALEB. Thunder, I know you ain't, Emmer. I was on'y jokin'.

EMMA. And I never doubted you them two years; and I won't when you sail away again, neither.

CALEB (*with a twinkle in his eye*). No, even a woman'd find it hard to git jealous of a whale!

EMMA (*laughing*). I wasn't thinking of whales, silly! But there's plenty of diversion going on in the ports you touched, if you'd a mind for it.

CALEB. Waal, I didn't have no mind for it, that's sartin. My fust vige as skipper, you don't s'pose I had time for no monkey-shinin', do ye ? Why, I was that anxious to bring back your Pa's ship with a fine vige that'd make him piles o' money. I didn't even think of nothin' else.

EMMA. 'Cepting me, I hope ?

CALEB. O' course ! What was my big aim in doin' it if it wasn't so's we'd git married when I come to home ? And then, s'far as ports go, we didn't tech at one the last year—'ceptin' when that durn tempest blowed us south and we put in at one o' the islands for water.

EMMA. What island ? You never told me nothing about that.

CALEB (*growing suddenly very embarrassed as if some memory occurred to him*). Ain't nothin' to tell, that's why. Just an island near the Line, that's all. On'y naked heathen livin' there—brown coloured savages that ain't even Christians. (*He gets to his feet abruptly and pulls out his watch.*) Gittin' late, must be. I got to go down to the store and git some things for Harriet afore I forgets 'em.

EMMA (*rising also and putting her hands on his shoulders*). But you did think of me and miss me all the time you was gone, didn't you ?—same as I did you.

CALEB. 'Course I did. Every minute.

EMMA (*nestling closer to him—softly*). I'm glad of that, Caleb. Well, good-bye for a little while.

CALEB. I'll step in again for a spell afore supper— that is, if you want me to.

EMMA. Yes, course I do, Caleb. Good-bye. (*She lifts her face to his.*)

CALEB. Good-bye, Emmer.

> (*He kisses her and holds her in his arms for a moment. Jack comes up the walk to the screen door. They do not notice his approach.*)

JACK (*peering in and seeing them—in a joking bellow*). Belay there !

> (*They separate with startled exclamations. Jack comes in grinning. He is a hulking stocky-built young fellow of 25. His heavy face is sunburned, handsome in a coarse, good-natured, animal fashion. His small blue eyes twinkle with the unconsciously malicious humour of the born practical joker. He wears thigh sea-boots turned down from the knees, dirty cotton shirt and pants, and a yellow sou'wester pushed jauntily on the back of his head, revealing his dishevelled, curly blonde hair. He carries a string of cod heads.*)

JACK (*laughing at the embarrassed expression on their faces*). Caught ye that time, by gum ! Go ahead ! Kiss her again, Caleb. Don't mind me.

EMMA (*with flurried annoyance*). You got a head on you just like one of them cod heads you're carrying —that stupid ! I should think you'd be ashamed at your age—shouting to scare folks as if you was a little boy.

JACK (*putting his arm about her waist*). There,

kitty, don't git to spittin'. (*Stroking her hair.*) Puss, puss, puss! Nice kitty! (*He laughs.*)

EMMA (*forced to smile—pushing him away*). Get away! You'll never get sense. Land sakes, what a brother to have!

JACK. Oh, I dunno. I ain't so bad, as brothers go—eh, Caleb?

CALEB (*smiling*). I reckon you'll do, Jack.

JACK. See there! Listen to Caleb. You got to take his word—love, honour, and *obey*, ye know, Emmer.

EMMA (*laughing*). Leave it to men folks to stick up for each other, right or wrong.

JACK (*cockily*). Waal, I'm willin' to leave it to the girls, too. Ask any of 'em you knows if I ain't a jim-dandy to have for a brother. (*He winks at Caleb who grins back at him.*)

EMMA (*with a sniff*). I reckon you don't play much brother with them—the kind you knows. You may fool 'em into believing you're some pumpkins, but they'd change their minds if they had to live in the same house with you playing silly jokes all the time.

JACK (*provokingly*). A good lot on 'em 'd be on'y too damn glad to git me in the same house—if I was fool enough to git married.

EMMA. "Pride goeth before a fall." But what's the good paying any attention to you. (*She smiles at him affectionately.*)

JACK (*exaggeratedly*). You see, Caleb? See how she misuses me—her lovin' brother. Now you know what you'll be up against for the rest o' your natural days.

CALEB. Don't see no way but what I got to bear it, Jack.

EMMA. Caleb needn't fear. He's diff'rent.

JACK (*with a sudden guffaw*). Oh, hell, yes! I was forgittin'. Caleb's a Sunday go-to-meetin' Saint, ain't he? Yes, he is!

EMMA (*with real resentment*). He's better'n what you are, if that's what you mean.

JACK (*with a still louder laugh*). Ho-ho! Caleb's one o' them goody-goody heroes out o' them story books you're always readin', ain't he?

CALEB (*soberly—a bit disturbed*). I was tellin' Emmer not to take me that high.

JACK. No use, Caleb. She won't hear of it. She's got her head set t'other way. You'd ought to heard her argyin' when you was gone about what a parson's pet you was. Butter won't melt in your mouth, no siree! Waal, love is blind—and deaf, too, as the feller says—and I can't argy no more 'cause I got to give Ma these heads. (*He goes to the door on right —then glances back at his sister maliciously and says meaningly.*) You ought to have a talk with Jim Benson, Emmer. Oughtn't she, Caleb. (*He winks ponderously and goes off laughing uproariously.*)

CALEB (*his face worried and angry*). Jack's a durn fool at times, Emmer,—even if he is your brother. He needs a good lickin'.

EMMA (*staring at him—uneasily*). What'd he mean about Jim Benson, Caleb?

212

CALEB (*frowning*). I don't know—exzactly. Makin' up foolishness for a joke, I reckon.

EMMA. You don't know—*exactly?* Then there is —something?

CALEB (*quickly*). Not as I know on. On'y Jim Benson's one o' them slick jokers, same's Jack; can't keep their mouths shet or mind their own business.

EMMA. Jim Benson was mate with you this last trip, wasn't he?

CALEB. Yes.

EMMA. Didn't him and you get along?

CALEB (*a trifle impatiently*). 'Course we did. Jim's all right. We got along fust rate. He just can't keep his tongue from waggin', that's all's the matter with him.

EMMA (*uneasily*). What's it got to wag about? You ain't done nothing wrong, have you?

CALEB. Wrong? No, nothin' a man'd rightly call wrong.

EMMA. Nothing you'd be shamed to tell me?

CALEB (*awkwardly*). Why—no, Emmer.

EMMA (*pleadingly*). You'd swear that, Caleb?

CALEB (*hesitating for a second—then firmly*). Yes, I'd swear. I'd own up to everything fair and square I'd ever done, if it comes to that p'int. I ain't shamed o' anything I ever done, Emmer. On'y—women folks ain't got to know everything, have they?

EMMA (*turning away from him—frightenedly*). Oh, Caleb!

CALEB (*preoccupied with his own thoughts—going to the door in rear*). I'll see you later, Emmer. I got to go up street now more'n ever. I want te give that Jim Benson a talkin' to he won't forgit in a hurry—that is, if he's been tellin' tales. Good-bye, Emmer.

EMMA (*faintly*). Good-bye, Caleb. (*He goes out. She sits in one of the rockers by the table, her face greatly troubled, her manner nervous and uneasy. Finally she makes a decision, goes quickly to the door on the right and calls.*) Jack! Jack!

JACK (*from the kitchen*). What you want?

EMMA. Come here a minute, will you?

JACK. Jest a second. (*She comes back by the table, fighting to conceal her agitation. After a moment Jack comes in from the right. He has evidently been washing up, for his face is red and shiny, his hair wet. He looks around for Caleb.*) Where's Caleb?

EMMA. He had to go up street. (*Then coming to the point abruptly—with feigned indifference.*) What's that joke about Jim Benson, Jack? It seemed to get Caleb all riled up.

JACK (*with a chuckle*). You got to ask Caleb about that, Emmer.

EMMA. I did. He didn't seem to want to own up it was anything.

JACK (*with a laugh*). 'Course he wouldn't. He don't 'preciate a joke when it's on him.

EMMA. How'd you come to hear of it?

JACK. From Jim. Met him this afternoon and me

214

and him had a long talk. He was tellin' me all 'bout their vige.

EMMA. Then it was on the vige this joke happened?

JACK. Yes. It was when they put in to git water at them South Islands where the tempest blowed 'em.

EMMA. Oh. (*Suspiciously*.) Caleb didn't seem willing to tell me much about their touching there.

JACK (*chuckling*). 'Course he didn't. Wasn't I sayin' the joke's on him? (*Coming closer to her—in a low, confidential tone, chucklingly*.) We'll fix up a joke on Caleb, Emmer, what d'ye say?

EMMA (*tortured by foreboding—resolved to find out what is behind all this by hook or crook—forcing a smile*). All right, Jack. I'm willing.

JACK. Then I'll tell you what Jim told me. And you put it up to Caleb, see, and pertend you're madder'n hell. (*Unable to restrain his mirth*.) Ho! ho! It'll git him wild if you do that. On'y I didn't tell ye, mind! You heard it from someone else. I don't want to git Caleb down on me. And you'd hear about it from someone sooner or later 'cause Jim and the rest o' the boys has been tellin' the hull town.

EMMA (*taken aback—frowning*). So all the town knows about it?

JACK. Yes, and they're all laffin' at Caleb. Oh, it ain't nothin' so out o' the ordinary. Most o' the whalin' men hereabouts have run up against it in their time. I've heard Pa and all the others tellin' stories like it out o' their experience. On'y with

Caleb it ended up so damn funny! (*He laughs.*) Ho-ho! Jimminy!

EMMA (*in a strained voice*). Well, ain't you going to tell me?

JACK. I'm comin' to it. Waal, seems like they all went ashore on them islands to git water and the native brown women, all naked a'most, come round to meet 'em same as they always does—wantin' to swap for terbaccer and other tradin' stuff with straw mats and whatever other junk they'd got. Them brown gals was purty as the devil, Jim says—that is, in their heathen, outlandish way—and the boys got makin' up to 'em; and then, o' course, everything happened like it always does, and even after they'd got all the water they needed aboard, it took 'em a week to round up all hands from where they was foolin' about with them nigger women.

EMMA (*in anguish*). Yes—but Caleb—he ain't like them others. He's diff'rent.

JACK (*with a sly wink*). Oho, is he? I'm comin' to Caleb. Waal, seems s'if he kept aboard mindin' his own business and winkin' at what the boys was doin'. And one o' them gals—the purtiest on 'em, Jim says —she kept askin', where's the captain? She wouldn't have nothin' to do with any o' the others. She thought on'y the skipper was good enough for her, I reckon. So one night jest afore they sailed some o' the boys, bein' drunk on native rum they'd stole, planned to put up a joke on Caleb and on that brown gal, too. So they tells her the captain had sent for her and she was to swim right out and git aboard the

216

ship where he was waitin' for her alone. That part of it was true enough 'cause Caleb was alone, all hands havin' deserted, you might say.

EMMA (*letting an involuntary exclamation escape her*). Oh!

JACK. Waal, that fool brown gal b'lieved 'em and she swum right off, tickled to death. What happened between 'em when she got aboard, nobody knows. Some thinks one thing and some another. And I ain't sayin' nothin' 'bout it (*with a wink*) but I know damn well what I'd 'a done in Caleb's boots, and I guess he ain't the cussed old woman you makes him out. But that part of it's got nothin' to do with the joke nohow. The joke's this : that brown gal took an awful likin' to Caleb and when she saw the ship was gittin' ready to sail she raised ructions, standin' on the beach howlin' and screamin', and beatin' her chest with her fists. And when they ups anchor, she dives in the water and swims out after 'em. There's no wind hardly and she kin swim like a fish and catches up to 'em and tries to climb aboard. At fust, Caleb tries to treat her gentle and argy with her to go back. But she won't listen, she gits wilder and wilder, and finally he gits sick of it and has the boys push her off with oars while he goes and hides in the cabin. Even this don't work. She keeps swimmin' round and yellin' for Caleb. And finally they has to p'int a gun at her and shoot in the water near her afore the crazy cuss gives up and swims back to home, howlin' all the time. (*With a chuckle.*) And Caleb lyin' low in the cabin skeered to move out, and all hands splittin' their sides! Gosh, I wish I'd been there! It must have been funnier'n hell! (*He laughs loudly—then noticing his sister's stony expression, stops abruptly.*) What're you pullin' that long face for, Emmer? (*Offendedly.*) Hell, you're a nice one to tell a joke to!

EMMA (*after a pause—forcing the words out slowly*). Caleb's comin' back here, Jack. I want you to see him for me. I want you to tell him——

JACK. Not me! You got to play this joke on him yourself or it won't work.

EMMA (*tensely*). This ain't a joke, Jack—what I mean. I want you to tell him I've changed my mind and I ain't going to marry him.

JACK. What!

EMMA. I been thinking things over, tell him—and I take back my promise—and he can have back his ring—and I ain't going to marry him.

JACK (*flabbergasted—peering into her face anxiously*). Say—what the hell——? Are you tryin' to josh me, Emmer? Or are you gone crazy all of a sudden?

EMMA. I ain't joking nor crazy neither. You tell him what I said.

JACK (*vehemently*). I will like ———. Say, what's come over you, anyhow?

EMMA. My eyes are opened, that's all, and I ain't going to marry him.

JACK. Is it—'count of that joke about Caleb I was tellin' you?

EMMA (*her voice trembling*). It's 'count of some-

218

thing I got in my own head. What you told only goes to prove I was wrong about it.

JACK (*greatly perturbed now*). Say, what's the matter? Can't you take a joke? Are you mad at him 'count o' that brown gal?

EMMA. Yes, I am—and I ain't going to marry him and that's all there is to it.

JACK (*argumentatively*). Jealous of a brown heathen woman that ain't no better'n a nigger? God sakes, Emmer, I didn't think you was so big a fool. Why them kind o' women ain't women like you. They don't count like folks. They ain't Christians—nor nothin'!

EMMA. That ain't it. I don't care what they are.

JACK. And it wasn't Caleb, anyhow. It was all her fixin'. And how'd you know he had anything to do with her—like that? I ain't said he did. Jim couldn't swear he did neither. And even if he did— what difference does it make? It ain't rightly none o' your business what he does on a vige. He didn't ask her to marry him, did he?

EMMA. I don't care. He'd ought to have acted diff'rent.

JACK. Oh, golly, there you go agen makin' a durned creepin' saint out of him! What d'you want to marry, anyhow—a man or a sky-pilot? Caleb's a man, ain't he?—and a damn good man and as smart a skipper as there be in these parts! What more d'you want, anyhow?

EMMA (*violently*). I want you to shet up! You're too dumb stupid and bad yourself to ever know what I'm thinking.

JACK (*resentfully*). Go to the devil, then! I'm goin' to tell Ma and set her on to you. You'll maybe listen to her and git some sense. (*He stamps out, right, while he is speaking. Emma bursts into sobs and throws herself on a chair, covering her face with her hands. Harriet Williams and Alfred Rogers come up the path to the door in rear. Peering through the screen and catching sight of Emma, Harriet calls.*) Emmer!

> (*Emma leaps to her feet and dabs at her eyes with a handkerchief in a vain effort to conceal traces of her tears. Harriet has come in, followed by Rogers. Caleb's sister is a tall, dark girl of twenty. Her face is plainly homely and yet attracts the eye by a certain boldly-appealing vitality of self-confident youth. She wears an apron and has evidently just come out of the kitchen. Rogers is a hefty young fisherman of 24, washed and got up in his ill-fitting best.*)

ROGERS. Hello, Emmer.

EMMA (*huskily, trying to force a smile*). Hello, Harriet. Hello, Alfred. Won't you set?

HARRIET. No, I jest run over from the house a second to see if—— Where's Caleb, Emmer?

EMMA. He's gone up street.

HARRIET. And here I be waitin' in the kitchen for him to bring back the things so's I can start his supper. (*With a laugh and a roguish look at Rogers.*) Dearie me, it ain't no use dependin' on a man to remember nothin' when he's in love.

ROGERS (*putting his arm about her waist and giving her a squeeze—grinning*). How 'bout me? Ain't I in love and ain't I as reliable as an old hoss?

HARRIET. Oh, you! You're the worst of 'em all.

ROGERS. You don't think so. (*He tries to kiss her.*)

HARRIET. Stop it. Ain't you got no manners? What'll Emmer think?

ROGERS. Emmer can't throw stones. Her and Caleb is worser at spoonin' than what we are. (*Harriet breaks away from him laughingly and goes to Emma.*)

HARRIET (*suddenly noticing the expression of misery on Emma's face—astonished*). Why, Emmer Crosby, what's the matter? You look as if you'd lost your best friend.

EMMA (*trying to smile*). Nothing. It's nothing.

HARRIET. It is, too! Why, I do believe you've been crying!

EMMA. No, I ain't.

HARRIET. You have, too! (*Putting her arms about Emma.*) Goodness, what's happened? You and Caleb ain't had a tiff, have you, with your weddin' only two days off?

EMMA (*with quick, resentful resolution*). There ain't going to be any wedding.

HARRIET. What!

ROGERS (*pricking up his ears—inquisitively*). Huh?

EMMA. Not in two days nor no time.

HARRIET (*dumbfounded*). Why, Emmer Crosby,

221

whatever's got into you ?   You and Caleb must have had an awful set to !

ROGERS (*with a man-of-the-world attitude of cynicism*). Don't take her so dead serious, Harriet. Emmer'll git over it like you all does.

EMMA (*angrily*).   You shet up, Alf Rogers !

> (*Mrs. Crosby enters bustlingly from the right. She is a large, fat, florid woman of fifty. In spite of her two hundred and more pounds she is surprisingly active, and the passive, lazy expression of her round moon face is belied by her quick, efficient movements. She exudes an atmosphere of motherly good nature. She wears an apron on which she is drying her hands as she enters. Jack follows her into the room. He has changed to a dark suit, and is ready for " up street.")*

MRS CROSBY (*smiling at Harriet and Rogers*).   After noon, Harriet—and Alf.

HARRIET.   Afternoon, Ma.

ROGERS.   Afternoon.

JACK (*grinning*).   There she be, Ma. (*Points to Emma.*) Don't she look like she'd scratch a feller's eyes out !   Phew !   Look at her back curve !   Meow ?   Sptt-sptt !   Nice puss !

> (*He gives a vivid imitation of a cat fight at this last. Then he and Rogers roar with laughter and Harriet cannot restrain a giggle and Mrs. Crosby smiles.*

222

*Emma stares stonily before her as if she
didn't hear.)*

MRS. CROSBY (*good-naturedly*). Shet up your foolin', Jack.

JACK (*pretending to be hurt*). Nobody in this house kin take a joke. (*He grins and beckons to Rogers.*) Come along, Alf. You kin 'preciate a joke. Come on in here and I'll tell you.

> (*The grinning Rogers follows him into the next
> room, where they can be heard talking and
> laughing during the following scene.*)

MRS. CROSBY (*smiling, puts her arms around Emma*). Waal, Emmer, what's this foolishness Jack's been tellin' about——

EMMA (*resentfully*). It ain't foolishness, Ma. I've made up my mind. I tell you that right here and now.

MRS. CROSBY (*after a quick glance at her face—soothingly*). There, there! Let's set down and be comfortable. Me, I don't relish roostin' on my feet. (*She pushes Emma gently into a rocker—then points to a chair on the other side of the table.*) Set down, Harriet.

HARRIET (*torn between curiosity and a sense of being one too many*). Maybe I'd best go home and leave you two alone?

MRS. CROSBY. Bosh! Ain't you like one o' the family—Caleb's sister and livin' right next door ever since you was all children playin' together. We ain't got no secrets from you. Set down. (*Harriet does so with an uncertain glance at the frozen Emma. Mrs. Crosby has efficiently bustled another rocker beside her*

223

daughter's and sits down with a comfortable sigh.)
There. (*She reaches over and takes one of her daughter's hands in hers.*) And now, Emmer, what's all this fuss over? (*As Emma makes no reply.*) Jack says as you've sworn you was breakin' with Caleb. Is that true?

EMMA. Yes.

MRS. CROSBY. Hmm. Caleb don't know this yet, does he?

EMMA. No. I asked Jack to tell him when he comes back.

MRS. CROSBY. Jack says he won't.

EMMA. Then I'll tell him myself. Maybe that's better, anyhow. Caleb'll know what I'm driving at and see my reason (*bitterly*)—which nobody else seems to.

MRS. CROSBY. Hmm. You ain't tried me yet. (*After a pause.*) Jack was a dumb fool to tell you 'bout them goin's-on at them islands they teched. Ain't no good repeatin' sech things.

EMMA (*surprised*). Did you know about it before Jack——

MRS. CROSBY. Mercy, yes. Your Pa heard it from Jim Benson fust thing they landed here, and Pa told me that night.

EMMA (*resentfully*). And you never told me!

MRS. CROSBY. Mercy, no. Course I didn't. They's trouble enough in the world without makin' more. If you was like most folks I'd told it to you. Me, I thought it was a good joke on Caleb.

EMMA (*with a shudder*). It ain't a joke to me.

224

MRS. CROSBY. That's why I kept my mouth shet. I knowed you was touchy and diff'rent from most.

EMMA (*proudly*). Yes, I am diff'rent—and that's just what I thought Caleb was, too—and he ain't.

HARRIET (*breaking in excitedly*). Is it that story about Caleb and that heathen brown woman you're talking about? Is that what you're mad at Caleb for, Emmer?

MRS. CROSBY (*as Emma remains silent*). Yes, Harriet, that's it.

HARRIET (*astonished*). Why, Emmer Crosby, how can you be so silly? You don't s'pose Caleb took it serious, do you, and him makin' them fire shots round her to scare her back to land and get rid of her? Good gracious! (*A bit resentfully.*) I hope you ain't got it in your head my brother Caleb would sink so low as to fall in love serious with one of them critters?

EMMA (*harshly*). He might just as well.

HARRIET (*bridling*). How can you say sech a thing! (*Sarcastically.*) I ain't heard that Caleb offered to marry her, have you? Then you might have some cause—— But d'you s'pose he's ever give her another thought? Not Caleb! I know him better'n that. He'd forgot all about the hull thing before they was out o' sight of land, I'll bet, and if them fools hadn't started this story going, he'd never remembered it again.

MRS. CROSBY (*nodding*). That's jest it. Harriet's right, Emmer.

EMMA. Ma!

MRS. CROSBY. Besides, you don't know there was anythin' wrong happened. Nobody kin swear that for sartin. Ain't that so, Harriet?

HARRIET (*hesitating—then frankly*). I don't know. Caleb ain't no plaster saint and I reckon he's as likely to sin that way as any other man. He wasn't married then and I s'pose he thought he was free to do as he's a mind to till he was hitched up. Goodness sakes, Emmer, all the men thinks that—and a lot of 'em after they're married, too.

MRS. CROSBY. Harriet's right, Emmer. If you've been wide awake to all that's happened in this town since you was old enough to know, you'd ought to realise what men be.

HARRIET (*scornfully*). Emma'd ought to fallen in love with a minister, not a sailor. As for me, I wouldn't give much thought of a man that was too goody-goody to raise Cain once in a while—before he married me, I mean. Why, look at Alf Rogers, Emmer. I'm going to marry him some day, ain't I? But I know right well all the foolin' he's done—and still is doing, I expect. I ain't sayin' I like it, but I do like him, and I got to take him the way he is, that's all. If you're looking for saints, you got to die first and go to heaven. A girl'd never git married hereabouts if she expected too much.

MRS. CROSBY. Harriet's right, Emmer.

EMMA (*resentfully*). Maybe she is, Ma, from her side. I ain't claiming she's wrong. Her and me just looks at things diff'rent, that's all. And she can't understand the way I feel about Caleb

226

HARRIET. Well, there's one thing certain, Emmer. You won't find a man in a day's walk is any better'n Caleb—or as good.

EMMA (*wearily*). I know that, Harriet.

HARRIET. Then it's all right. You'll make up with him, and I s'pose I'm a fool to be takin' it so serious. (*As Emma shakes her head.*) Oh, yes, you will. You wouldn't want to get him all broke up, would you ? (*As Emma keeps silent—irritably.*) Story-book notions, that's the trouble with you, Emmer. You're gettin' to think you're better'n the rest of us.

EMMA (*vehemently*). No, I don't! Can't you see——

MRS. CROSBY. Thar, now! Don't you two git to fightin'—to make things worse.

HARRIET (*repentantly, coming and putting her arms around Emma and kissing her*). I'm sorry, Emmer. You know I wouldn't fall out with you for nothing or nobody, don't you ? Only it gits me riled to think of how awful broke up Caleb'd be if—— But you'll make it all up with him when he comes, won't you ?

> (*Emma stares stubbornly before her. Before she has a chance to reply a roar of laughter comes from the next room as Jack winds up his tale.*)

ROGERS (*from the next room*). Gosh, I wished I'd been there! (*He follows Jack into the room. Both are grinning broadly. Rogers says teasingly.*) Reckon I'll take to whalin' 'stead o' fishin' after this. You won't mind, Harriet ? From what I hears o' them

227

brown women, I'm missin' a hull lot by stayin' at home.

HARRIET (*in a joking tone—with a meaning glance at Emma*). Go on, then! There's plenty of fish in the sea. Anyhow, I'd never git jealous of your foolin' with one of them heathen critters. They ain't worth notice from a Christian.

JACK. Oho, ain't they! They're purty as pictures, Benson says. (*With a wink.*) And mighty accommodatin' in their ways. (*He and Rogers roar delightedly. Emma shudders with revulsion.*)

MRS. CROSBY (*aware of her daughter's feeling—smilingly but firmly*). Get out o' this, Jack. You, too, Alf. Go on up street if you want to joke. You're in my way.

JACK. Aw right, Ma. Come on up street, Alf.

HARRIET. Wait. I'll go with you a step. I got to see if Caleb's got back with them supper things. (*They all go to the door in rear. Jack and Rogers pass out, talking and laughing. Harriet turns in the doorway—sympathetically.*) I'll give Caleb a talking to before he comes over. Then it'll be easy for you to finish him. Treat him firm but gentle and you'll see he won't never do it again in a hurry. After all, he wasn't married, Emmer—and he's a man—and what can you expect? Good-bye. (*She goes.*)

EMMA (*inaudibly*). Good-bye.

MRS. CROSBY (*after a pause in which she rocks back and forth studying her daughter's face—placidly.*) Harriet's right, Emmer. You give him a good talkin'-to and he won't do it again.

228

EMMA (*coldly*). I don't care whether he does or not. I ain't going to marry him.

MRS. CROSBY (*uneasy—persuasively*). Mercy, you can't act like that, Emmer. Here's the weddin' on'y two days off, and everythin' fixed up with the minister, and your Pa and Jack has bought new clothes speshul for it, and I got a new dress——

EMMA (*turning to her mother—pleadingly*). You wouldn't want me to keep my promise to Caleb if you knew I'd be unhappy, would you, Ma?

MRS. CROSBY (*hesitatingly*). N-no, Emmer. (*Then decisively.*) 'Course I wouldn't. It's because I know he'll make you happy. (*As Emma shakes her head.*) Shaw, Emmer, you can't tell me you've got over all likin' for him jest 'count o' this one foolishness o' his'n.

EMMA. I don't love him—what he is now. I loved—what I thought he was.

MRS. CROSBY (*more and more uneasy*). That's all your queer notions, and I don't know where you gits them from. Caleb ain't changed, neither have you. Why, Emmer, it'd be jest like goin' agen an act of Nature for you not to marry him. Ever since you was children you been livin' side by side, goin' round together, and neither you nor him ever did seem to care for no one else. Bosh, Emmer, you'll git me to lose patience with you if you act that stubborn. You'd ought to remember all he's been to you and forget this one little wrong he's done.

EMMA. I can't, Ma. It makes him another person —not Caleb, but someone just like all the others.

MRS. CROSBY. Waal, is the others so bad? Men is men the world over, I reckon.

EMMA. No, they ain't bad. I ain't saying that. Don't I like 'em all? If it was one of the rest—like Jim Benson or Jack, even—had done this I'd thought it was a joke, too. I ain't strict in judging 'em and you know it. But—can't you see, Ma?—Caleb always seemed diff'rent—and I thought he was.

MRS. CROSBY (*somewhat impatiently*). Waal, if he ain't, he's a good man jest the same, as good as any sensible girl'd want to marry.

EMMA (*slowly*). I don't want to marry nobody no more. I'll stay single.

MRS. CROSBY (*tauntingly*). An old maid! (*Then resentfully.*) Emmer, d'you s'pose if I'd had your high-fangled notions o' what men ought to be when I was your age, d'you s'pose you'd ever be settin' there now?

EMMA (*slowly*). No. I know from what I can guess from his own stories, Pa never was no saint.

MRS. CROSBY (*in a tone of finality, as if this settled the matter*). There, now! And ain't he been as good a husband to me as ever lived, and a good father to you and Jack? You'll find out Caleb'll turn out the same. You think it over. (*She gets up—bustlingly.*) And now I got to git back in the kitchen.

EMMA (*wringing her hands—desperately*). Oh, Ma, why can't you see what I feel? Of course, Pa's good—as good as good can be——

CAPTAIN CROSBY (*from outside the door, which he has*

230

approached without their noticing him—in a jovial bellow). What's that 'bout Pa bein' good? (*He comes in laughing. He is a squat, bow-legged, powerful man, almost as broad as he is long—sixty years old, but still in the prime of health and strength, with a great, red, weather-beaten face seamed by sun wrinkles. His sandy hair is thick and dishevelled. He is dressed in an old baggy suit much the worse for wear—striped cotton shirt open at the neck. He pats Emma on the back with a playful touch that almost jars her off her feet.*) Thunderin' Moses, that's the fust time ever I heerd good o' myself by listenin'! Most times it's: "Crosby? D'you mean that drunken, good-for-nothin', mangy old cuss?" That's what I hears usual. Thank ye, Emmer. (*Turning to his wife.*) What ye got to say now, Ma? Here's Emmer tellin' you the truth after you hair-pullin' me all these years 'cause you thought it wa'n't. I always told ye I was good, ain't I—good as hell I be! (*He shakes with laughter and kisses his wife a resounding smack.*)

MRS. CROSBY (*teasing lovingly*). Emmer don't know you like I do.

CROSBY (*turning back to Emma again*). Look-a-here, Emmer, I jest seen Jack. He told me some fool story 'bout you fallin' out with Caleb. Reckon he was joshin' wa'n't he?

MRS. CROSBY (*quickly*). Oh, that's all settled, John. Don't you go stirrin' it up again. (*Emma seems about to speak, but stops helplessly after one glance at her father.*)

CROSBY. An' all 'count o' that joke they're tellin'

231

'bout him and that brown female critter, Jack says. Hell, Emmer, you ain't a real Crosby if you takes a joke like that serious. Thunderin' Moses, what the hell d'you want Caleb to be—a durned, he-virgin, missionary? Caleb's a man wo'th ten o' most, and, spite o' his bein' on'y a boy yit, he's the smartest skipper out o' this port and you'd ought to be proud you'd got him. And as for them islands, all whalin' men knows 'em. I've teched thar for water more'n once myself, and I know them brown females like a book. And I tells you, after a year or more aboard ship, a man'd have to be a goll-durned geldin' if he don't——

MRS. CROSBY (*glancing uneasily at Emma*). Ssshh! You come out in the kitchen with me, Pa, and leave Emmer be.

CROSBY. God A'mighty, Ma, I ain't sayin' nothin' agen Emmer, be I? I knows Emmer ain't that crazy. If she ever got religion that bad, I'd ship her off as female missionary to the damned yellow Chinks. (*He laughs.*)

MRS. CROSBY (*taking his arm*). You come with me. I want to talk with you 'bout somethin'.

CROSBY (*going*). Aye-aye, skipper! You're boss aboard here. (*He goes out right with her, laughing. Emma stands for a while, staring stonily before her. She sighs hopelessly, clasping and unclasping her hands, looking around the room as if she longed to escape from it. Finally she sits down helplessly and remains fixed in a strained attitude, her face betraying the conflict that is tormenting her. Slow steps sound from the path*

232

in front of the house. Emma recognises them and her face freezes into an expression of obstinate intolerance. Caleb appears outside the screen door. He looks in, coughs—then asks uncertainly.) It's me, Emmer. Kin I come in?

EMMA (*coldly*). Yes

CALEB (*comes in and walks down beside her chair. His face is set emotionlessly, but his eyes cannot conceal a worried bewilderment, a look of uncomprehending hurt. He stands uncomfortably, fumbling with his hat, waiting for her to speak or look up. As she does neither, he finally blurts out*). Kin I set a while?

EMMA (*in the same cold tone*). Yes. (*He lowers himself carefully to a wooden posture on the edge of a rocker near hers.*)

CALEB (*after a pause*). I seen Jim Benson. I give him hell. He won't tell no more tales, I reckon. (*Another pause.*) I stepped in home on the way back from the store. I seen Harriet. She says Jack'd told you that story they're all tellin' as a joke on me. (*Clenching his fists—angrily.*) Jack's a durn fool. He needs a good lickin' from someone.

EMMA (*resentfully*). Don't try to put the blame on Jack. He only told me the truth, didn't he? (*Her voice shows that she hopes against hope for a denial.*)

CALEB (*after a long pause—regretfully*). Waal, I guess what he told is true enough.

EMMA (*wounded*). Oh!

CALEB. But that ain't no good reason for tellin' it. Them sort o' things ought to be kept among

233

men. (*After a pause—gropingly.*) I didn't want
nothin' like that to happen, Emmer. I didn't mean
it to. I was thinkin' o' how you might feel—even
down there. That's why I stayed aboard all the
time when the boys was ashore. I wouldn't have
b'lieved it could happen—not to me. (*A pause.*) I
wish you could see them islands, Emmer, and be there
for a time. Then you might see—— It's hard's hell
to explain, and you havin' never seen 'em. Everything is diff'rent down there—the weather, and the
trees and water. You git lookın' at it all, and you
git to feel diff'rent from what you do at home here.
It's purty hereabouts sometimes—like now, in spring
—but it's purty there all the time—and down there
you notice it and you git feelin'—diff'rent. And
them native women—they're diff'rent. A man don't
think of 'em as women—like you. But they're purty
—in their fashion—and at night they sings—and it's
all diff'rent like something you'd see in a painted
picture. (*A pause.*) That night when she swum
out and got aboard when I was alone, she caught me
by s'prise. I wasn't expectin' nothin' o' that sort. I
tried to make her git back to land at fust—but she
wouldn't go. She couldn't understand enough English
for me to tell her how I felt—and I reckon she wouldn't
have seed my p'int anyhow, her bein' a native. (*A
pause.*) And then I was afeerd she'd catch cold
goin' round all naked and wet in the moonlight—
though it was warm—and I wanted to wrap a blanket
round her. (*He stops as if he had finished.*)

EMMA (*after a long, tense pause—dully*). Then you
own up—there really was something happened ?

234

CALEB (*after a pause*). I was sorry for it, after. I locked myself in the cabin and left her to sleep out on deck.

EMMA (*after a pause—fixedly*). I ain't going to marry you, Caleb.

CALEB. Harriet said you'd said that ; but I didn't b'lieve you'd let a slip like that make—such a diff'rence.

EMMA (*with finality*). Then you can believe it now, Caleb.

CALEB (*after a pause*). You got queer, strict notions, Emmer. A man'll never live up to 'em—with never one slip. But you got to act accordin' to your lights, I expect. It sort o' busts everythin' to bits for me—— (*His voice betrays his anguish for a second, but he instantly regains his iron control.*) But o' course, if you ain't willin' to take me the way I be, there's nothin' to do. And whatever you think is best, suits me.

EMMA (*after a pause—gropingly*). I wish I could explain my side of it—so's you'd understand. I ain't got any hard feelings against you, Caleb—not now. It ain't plain jealousy—what I feel. It ain't even that I think you've done nothing terrible wrong. I think I can understand—how it happened—and make allowances. I know that most any man would do the same, and I guess all of 'em I ever met has done it.

CALEB (*with a glimmer of eager hope*). Then— you'll forgive it, Emmer ?

EMMA. Yes, I forgive it. But don't think that my

235

forgiving is going to make any diff'rence—'cause I
ain't going to marry you, Caleb. That's final. (*After
a pause—intensely.*) Oh, I wish I could make you
see—my reason. You don't. You never will, I
expect. What you done is just what any other man
would have done—and being like them is exactly
what'll keep you from ever seeing my meaning. (*After
a pause—in a last effort to make him understand.*)
Maybe it's my fault more'n your'n. It's like this,
Caleb. Ever since we was little I guess I've always
had the idea that you was—diff'rent. And when we
growed up and got engaged I thought that more and
more. And you was diff'rent, too! And that was
why I loved you. And now you've proved you ain't.
And so how can I love you any more? I don't,
Caleb, and that's all there is to it. You've busted
something way down inside me—and I can't love
you no more.

CALEB (*gloomily*). I've warned you often, ain't
I, you was settin' me up where I'd no business to be.
I'm human like the rest and always was. I ain't
diff'rent. (*After a pause—uncertainly.*) I reckon there
ain't no use sayin' nothing' more. I'll go home.
(*He starts to rise.*)

EMMA. Wait. I don't want you to go out of
here with no hard feelings. You 'n' me, Caleb, we've
been too close all our lives to ever get to be enemies.
I like you, Caleb, same's I always did. I want us to
stay friends. I want you to be like one of the family
same's you've always been. There's no reason you
can't. I don't blame you—as a man—for what I
236

wouldn't hold against any other man. If I find I can't love you—that way—no more or be your wife, it's just that I've decided—things being what they be and me being what I am—I won't marry no man. I'll stay single. (*Forcing a smile.*) I guess there's worse things than being an old maid.

CALEB. I can't picture you that, Emmer. It's natural in some, but it ain't in you. (*Then with a renewal of hope.*) And o' course I want to stay friends with you, Emmer. There's no hard feelin's on my side. You got a right to your own way—even if—— (*Hopefully.*) And maybe if I show you what I done wasn't natural to me—by never doin' it again—maybe the time'll come when you'll be willin' to forget——

EMMA (*shaking her head—slowly*). It ain't a question of time, Caleb. It's a question of something being dead. And when a thing's died, time can't make no diff'rence.

CALEB (*sturdily*). You don't know that for sure, Emmer. You're human, too, and as liable to make mistakes as any other. Maybe you on'y think it's dead, and when I come back from the next vige and you've had two years to think it over, you'll see diff'rent and know I ain't as bad as I seem to ye now.

EMMA (*helplessly*). But you don't seem bad, Caleb. And two years can't make no change in me—that way.

CALEB (*feeling himself somehow more and more heartened by hope*). I ain't givin' up hope, Emmer, and you can't make me. Not by a hell of a sight,

237

(*With emphasis.*) I ain't never goin' to marry no woman but you, Emmer. You can trust my word for that. And I'll wait for ye to change your mind, I don't care a durn how long it'll take—till I'm sixty years old—thirty years if it's needful! (*He rises to his feet as he is speaking this last.*)

EMMA (*with a mournful smile*). You might just as well say for life, Caleb. In thirty years we'll both be dead and gone, probably. And I don't want you to think it's needful for you to stay single 'cause I——

CALEB. I ain't goin' to stay single. I'm goin' to wait for you. And some day when you realise men was never cut out for angels you'll——

EMMA (*helplessly*). Me 'n' you'll never understand each other, Caleb, so long as we live. (*Getting up and holding out her hand.*) Good-bye, Caleb. I'm going up and lie down a while.

CALEB (*made hopeless again by her tone—clasps her hand mechanically—dully*). Good-bye, Emmer. (*He goes to the door in the rear, opens it, then hesitates and looks back at her as she goes out the door on the right without turning around. Suddenly he blurts out despairingly.*) You'll remember what I told ye 'bout waitin', Emmer ?

> (*She is gone, makes no reply. His face sets in its concealment mask of emotionlessness and he turns slowly and goes out the door as*

THE CURTAIN FALLS

Diff'rent
Act Two

Act Two

Thirty years after—the scene is the same but not the same. The room has a grotesque aspect of old age turned flighty and masquerading as the most empty-headed youth. There is an obstreperous newness about everything. Orange curtains are at the windows. The carpet has given way to a varnished hardwood floor, its glassy surface set off by three small, garish-coloured rugs, placed with precision in front of the two doors and under the table. The wall-paper is now a cream colour sprayed with pink flowers. Eye-aching seascapes, of the painted-to-order quality, four in number, encased in gilded frames, are hung on the walls at mathematically spaced intervals. The plush-covered chairs are gone, replaced by a set of varnished oak. The horse-hair sofa has been relegated to the attic. A cane-bottomed affair with fancy cushions serves in its stead. A gramophone is where the old mahogany chest had been. A brand new piano shines re-splendently in the far right corner by the door, and a bookcase with glass doors that pull up and slide in, flanks the fireplace. This bookcase is full of instalment-plan sets of uncut volumes. The table at centre is of varnished oak. On it are piles of fashion magazines and an electric reading lamp. Only the old Bible, which still preserves its place of honour on the table, and the marble clock on the mantel, have survived the renovation and serve to emphasise it all the more by contrast.

It is late afternoon of a day in the early spring of the year 1920.

As the curtain rises, Emma and Benny Rogers are discovered. She is seated in a rocker by the table. He is standing by the gramophone which is playing a jazz band record. He whistles, goes through the motions of dancing to the music. He is a young fellow of twenty-three, a replica of his father in Act One, but coarser, more hardened and cocksure. He is dressed in the khaki uniform of a private in the United States Army. The thirty years have transformed Emma into a withered, scraggy woman. But there is something revoltingly incongruous about her, a pitiable sham, a too-apparent effort to cheat the years by appearances. The white dress she wears is too frilly, too youthful for her; so are the high-heeled shoes and clocked silk stockings. There is an absurd suggestion of rouge on her tight cheeks and thin lips, of pencilled make-up about her eyes. The black of her hair is brazenly untruthful. Above all there is shown in her simpering, self-consciously coquettish manner that laughable—and at the same time irritating and disgusting—mockery of undignified age snatching greedily at the empty similitude of youth. She resembles some passé

242

stock actress of fifty made up for a heroine of twenty.

BENNY (*as the record stops—switches off the machine*). Oh, baby! Some jazz!

EMMA (*smiling lovingly at his back*). I'm glad you like it. It's one of them you picked out on the list.

BENNY. Oh, I'm a smart little picker, aw right. (*Turning to her.*) Say, you're a regular feller—gettin' them records for me.

EMMA (*coquettishly*). Well, if that ain't just like a man! Who told you I git them just for you?

BENNY. Well, didn't you?

EMMA. No indeed! I only took your advice on what to get. I knew you'd know, being growed to a man of the world now since you was overseas. But I got 'em because I like them jazz tunes myself. They put life and ginger in an old lady like me—not like them slow, old-time tunes.

BENNY (*bends over chair—kiddingly*). You ain't old. That's all bunk.

EMMA (*flattered*). Now, now, Benny!

BENNY. You ain't. You're a regular up-to-date sport—the only live one in this dead dump. (*With a grin.*) And if you fall for that jazz stuff, all you got to do now is learn to dance to it.

EMMA (*giggling*). I will—if you'll teach me.

BENNY (*struggling with a guffaw*). Oh, oui! Sure i will. We'll have a circus, me an' you. Say, you're sure one of the girls aw right, Aunt Emmer.

EMMA. Oh, you needn't think we're *all* so behind

243

the times at home here just because you've been to France and all over.

BENNY. *You* ain't, I'll say, Aunt Emmer.

EMMA. And how often have I got to tell you not to call me Aunt Emmer?

BENNY (*with a grin*). Oh, oui! My foot slipped. 'Scuse me, Emmer.

EMMA (*delighted by his coarse familiarity*). That's better. Why, you know well enough I ain't your aunt anyway.

BENNY. I got to get used to the plain Emmer. They taught me to call you " aunt " when I was a kid. (*Emma looks displeased at this remark and Benny hastens to add cajolingly.*) And you almost was my aunt-in-law one time from what I've heard. (*Winks at her cunningly.*)

EMMA (*flustered*). That was ages ago. (*Catching herself quickly.*) Not so awful long really, but it's all so dead and gone it seems a long while.

BENNY (*unthinkingly*). It was before I was born, wasn't it? (*Seeing her expression he hurries on.*) Well, that ain't so darned long. Say, here's something I never could make out—how did you ever come to fall for Uncle Caleb?

EMMA (*bridling—quickly*). I never did. That's all talk, Benny. We was good friends and still are. I was young and foolish and got engaged to him—and then discovered I didn't like him that way. That's all there ever was to it.

BENNY (*resentfully*). I can't figure how anybody'd ever like him anyway. He's a darn stingy,

244

ugly old cuss, if you want my opinion of him. I can't stand him at all. I've hated him ever since Pa died and Ma and me had to go live next door to him.

EMMA. You oughtn't to say that. He's kind at bottom, spite of his rough ways, and he's brought you up.

BENNY (*grumpily*). Dragged me up, you mean. (*With a calculating look at her out of the corners of his eyes.*) He's a tight-wad and I hate folks that're tight with their coin. Spend and be a good sport, that's my motto. (*Flattering.*) He'd ought to be more like you that way, Emmer.

EMMA (*pleased—condescendingly*). Your Uncle Caleb's an old man, remember. He's set in his ways and believes in being strict with you—too strict, I've told him.

BENNY. He's got piles of money hoarded in the bank, but he's too mean even to retire from whalin' himself—goes right on makin' vige after vige to grab more and never spends a penny less'n he has to. It was always like pryin' open a safe for me to separate him from a cent. (*With extreme disgust.*) Aw, he's a miser. I hate him and I always did!

EMMA (*looking towards the door apprehensively*). Ssshh!

BENNY. What you scared of? He don't get in from New Bedford till the night train and even if he's got to the house by this he'll be busy as a cock bird for an hour getting himself dolled up to pay you a call.

EMMA (*perfunctorily*). I hope he's had a good vige and is in good health.

BENNY (*roughly*). You needn't worry. He's too

mean ever to get real sick. Gosh, I wish Pa'd lived—
or Uncle Jack. They wasn't like him. I was only
a kid when they got drowned, but I remember enough
about 'em to know they was good sports. Wasn't they?

EMMA (*rather primly*). They was too sporty for
their own good.

BENNY. Don't you hand me that. That don't
sound like you. You're a sport yourself. (*After a
pause.*) Say, it's nutty when you come to think of
it—Uncle Caleb livin' next door all these years and
comin' to call all the time when he ain't at sea.

EMMA. What's funny about that? We've always
been good friends.

BENNY (*with a grin*). It's just as if the old guy
was still mashin' you. And I'll bet anything he's
as stuck on you as he ever was—the old fool!

EMMA (*with a coquettish titter*). Gracious, Benny,
a body'd think you were actually jealous of your
uncle the way you go on.

BENNY (*with a mocking laugh*). Jealous! Oh, oui!
Sure I am! Kin you blame me? (*Then seriously,
with a calculating look at her.*) No, all kiddin' aside,
I know he'll run me down first second he sees you.
Ma'll tell him all her tales, and he'll be sore at me
right off. He's always hated me anyway He was
glad when I enlisted, 'cause that got him rid of me.
All he was hopin' was that some German'd get me for
good. Then when I come back he wouldn't do
nothin' for me so I enlisted again.

EMMA (*chiding—playfully*). Now, Benny! Didn't
you tell me you enlisted again 'cause you were sick o'
246

this small place and wanted to be out where there was more fun ?

BENNY. Well o' course it was that, too. But I could have a swell time even in this dump if he'd loosen out and give me a bit. (*Again with the calculating look at her.*) Why, look here, right now there's a pal of mine wants me to meet him in Boston and he'll show me a good time, and if I had a hundred dollars——

EMMA. A hundred dollars ! That's an awful lot to spend, Benny.

BENNY (*disgustedly*). Now you're talkin' tight like him.

EMMA (*hastily*). Oh, no, Benny. You know better'n that. What was you sayin'—if you had a hundred dollars——?

BENNY. That ain't such a deal these days with everything gone up so. If I went to Boston I'd have to get dolled up and everything. And this pal of mine is a sport and a spender. Easy come, easy go is his motto. His folks ain't tight 'uns like mine. And I couldn't show myself up by travellin' 'round with him and just spongin' on him. (*With the calculating glance to see what effect his words are having—pretending to dismiss the subject.*) But what's the good of talkin' ? I got some hopes tellin' that to Uncle Caleb. He'd give me one look and then put a double padlock on his purse. But it ain't fair just the same. Here I'm sweatin' blood in the army after riskin' my life in France and when I get a leave to home, everyone treats me like an unwanted dog.

247

EMMA (*softly*). Do you mean me, too, Benny?

BENNY—No, not you. You're diff'rent from the rest. You're regular—and you ain't any of my real folks either, and ain't got any reason.

EMMA (*coquettishly*). Oh, yes, I have a reason. I like you very, very much, Benny—better than anyone in the town—especially since you've been home these last few times and come to call so often and I feel I've growed to know you. When you first came back from France I never would have recognised you as Harriet's Benny, you was so big and strong and handsome.

BENNY (*uncomfortably*). Aw, you're kiddin'. But you can tell how good I think you are from me bein' over here so much—so you know I ain't lyin'. (*Made more and more uncomfortable by the ardent looks Emma is casting at him.*) Well, guess I'll be movin' along.

EMMA (*pleadingly*). Oh, you mustn't go yet! Just when we're gettin' so friendly!

BENNY. Uncle Caleb'll be over soon and I don't want him to catch me here—nor nowhere else till he gets calmed down after hearin' Ma's kicks about me. So I guess I better get up street.

EMMA. He won't come for a long time yet. I know when to expect him. (*Pleading ardently and kittenishly.*) Do set down a while, Benny! Lord, I hardly get a sight of you before you want to run away again. I'll begin to think you're only pretending to like me.

BENNY (*seeing his calculations demand it*). Aw right —jest for a second. (*He looks about him, seeking a*
248

neutral subject for conversation.) Gee, you've had this old place fixed up swell since I was home last.

EMMA (*coquettishly*). Guess who I had it all done for, mostly ?

BENNY. For yourself, of course.

EMMA (*shaking her head roguishly*). No, not for me, not for me ! Not that I don't like it, but I'd never have gone to the trouble and expense for myself. (*With a sigh.*) I s'pose poor Ma and Pa turned over in their graves when I ordered it to be done.

BENNY (*with a sly grin*). Who d'you have it done for, then ?

EMMA. For you ! Yes, for you, Benny—so's you'd have a nice up-to-date place to came to when you was on vacation from the horrid old army.

BENNY (*embarrassed*). Well, it's quite aw right. And it sure looks swell—nothing cheap about it.

EMMA (*delighted*). As long as you like it, I'm satisfied. (*Then suddenly, wagging an admonishing finger at him and hiding beneath a joking manner an undercurrent of uneasiness.*) I was forgetting I got a bone to pick with you, young man ! I heard them sayin' at the store that you'd been up callin' on that Tilly Small evenin' before last.

BENNY (*with a lady-killer's carelessness*). Aw, I was passin' by and she called me in, that's all.

EMMA (*frowning*). They said you had the piano goin' and was singing and no end of high jinks.

BENNY. Aw, these small town folk think you're raising hell if you're up after eleven.

EMMA (*excitedly*). I ain't blamin' you. But her

249

—she ought to have better sense—at her age, too, when she's old enough to be your mother.

BENNY. Aw, say, she ain't half as old——(*Catching himself.*) Oh, she's an old fool, you're right there, Emmer.

EMMA (*severely*). And I hope you know the kind of woman she is and has been since she was a girl.

BENNY (*with a wink*). I wasn't born yesterday. I got her number long ago. I ain't in my cradle, get me! I'm in the army! Oui! (*Chuckles.*)

EMMA (*fidgeting nervously*). What'd you—what'd you do when you was there?

BENNY. Why, nothing'. I told her to cut the rough work and behave—and a nice time was had by all. (*He grins provokingly.*)

EMMA (*springs to her feet nervously*). I don't know what to think—when you act so queer about it.

BENNY (*carelessly*). Well, don't think nothing wrong—'cause there wasn't. Bill Tinker was with me and we was both wishin' we had a drink. And Bill says, "Let's go see Tilly Small. She always has some buried and if we hand her a line of talk maybe she'll drag out the old bottle." So we did—and she did. We kidded her for a couple of drinks. (*He snickers.*)

EMMA (*standing in front of him—fidgeting*). I want you to promise you won't go to see her no more. If you—if you want liquor now and again, maybe I—maybe I can fix it so's I can get some to keep here for you.

BENNY (*eagerly*). Say, that'd be great! Will you? (*She nods. He goes on carelessly.*) And sure I'll promise not to see Tilly no more. Gosh, what do you think I care about her? Or about any dame

250

in this town, for that matter—'ceptin' you. These small town skirts interest me nothin'. (*With a grin.*) You forgot I was in France—and after the dames over there these birds here look some guys.

EMMA (*sits down—wetting her lips*). And what—what are those French critters like?

BENNY (*with a wink*). Oh, boy! They're some pippins! It ain't so much that they're better lookin' as that they've got a way with 'em—lots of ways. (*He laughs with a lascivious smirk.*)

EMMA (*unconsciously hitches her chair nearer his. The turn the conversation has taken seems to have aroused a hectic, morbid intensity in her. She continually wets her lips and pushes back her hair from her flushed face as if it were stifling her.*) What do you mean, Benny? What kind of ways have they got—them French girls?

BENNY (*smirking mysteriously*). Oh, ways of dressin' and doin' their hair—and lots of ways.

EMMA (*eagerly*). Tell me! Tell me all about 'em. You needn't be scared—to talk open with me. I ain't as strict as I seem—about hearin' things. Tell me! I've heard French girls was awful wicked.

BENNY. I don't know about wicked, but they're darned good sports. They'd do anything a fellow asks 'em. Oui, tooty sweet! (*Laughs foolishly.*)

EMMA. And what—what'd you ask 'em, for instance?

BENNY (*with a wink*). Curiosity killed a cat! Ask me no questions and I'll tell you no lies.

EMMA (*with queer, stupid insistence*). But won't you tell me? Go on!

251

BENNY. Can't be did, Aunt Emmer, can't be did! (*With a silly laugh.*) You're too young. No, all I'll say is, that to the boys who've knocked around over there the girls in town here are just rank amatoors. They don't know how to love, and that's a fact. (*He gets to his feet.*) And as for an old dud like Tilly—not me! Well, I guess I'll get along——

EMMA (*getting up and putting a hand on his arm—feverishly*). No, don't go. Not yet—not yet. No, don't go.

BENNY (*stepping away with an expression of repulsion*). Why not? What's the matter with you, Aunt Emmer? You look 's if you was gettin' sick. (*Before she can reply, Harriet's voice is heard calling.*)

HARRIET. Benny! Benny! (*This acts like a pail of cold water on Emma who moves away from Benny quickly.*)

EMMA. That's Harriet. It's your Ma calling, Benny.

BENNY (*impatiently*). I know. That means Uncle Caleb has come and she's told him her stories and it's up to me to go catch hell. (*Stopping Emma as she goes towards the door as if to answer Harriet's hail.*) Don't answer, Aunt Emmer. Let her come over here to look. I want to speak to her and find out how I stand before he sees me.

EMMA (*doubtfully*). I don't know as she'll come. She's been actin' funny to me lately, Harriet has, and she ain't put her foot in my door the last month.

BENNY (*as his mother's voice is heard much nearer, calling " Benny! "*). There! Sure she's comin'.

EMMA (*flustered*). Gracious, I can't let her see me this way. I got to run upstairs and tidy myself a little. (*She starts for the door at right.*)

252

BENNY (*flatteringly*). Aw, you look swell. Them new clothes you got looks great.

EMMA (*turning in the doorway—coquettishly*). Oh, them French girls ain't the only ones knows how to fix up.

> (*She flounces out. Benny stands looking after her with a derisive grin of contempt. There is a sharp knock on the door in the rear. Benny goes to open it, his expression turning surly and sullen. Harriet enters. She wears an apron over her old-fashioned black dress with a brooch at the neck. Her hair is grey, her face thin, lined and careworn, with a fretful, continuously irritated expression. Her shoulders stoop, and her figure is flabby and ugly. She stares at her son with resentful annoyance.*)

HARRIET. Ain't you got sense enough, you big lump, to answer me when I call, and not have me shouting my lungs out?

BENNY. I never heard you callin'.

HARRIET. You're lyin' and you know it. (*Then severely.*) Your uncle's to home. He's waitin' to talk to you.

BENNY. Let him wait. (*In a snarling tone.*) I s'pose you've been givin' him an earful of lies about me?

HARRIET. I told him the truth, if that's what you mean. How you stole the money out of the bureau drawer——

253

BENNY (*alarmed, but pretending scorn*). Aw, you don't know it was me. You don't know nothin' about it.

HARRIET (*ignoring this*). And about your disgracin' him and me with your drunken carryin's-on with that harlot, Tilly Small, night after night.

BENNY. Aw, wha'd you know about that?

HARRIET. And last but not least, the sneakin' way you're makin' a silly fool out of poor Emmer Crosby.

BENNY (*with a grin*). You don't notice her kickin' about it, do you? (*Brusquely.*) Why don't you mind your own business, Ma?

HARRIET (*violently*). It's a shame, that's what it is! That I should live to see the day when a son of mine'd descend so low he'd tease an old woman to get money out of her, and her alone in the world. Oh, you're low, you're low all through like your Pa was—and since you been in the army you got bold so you ain't even ashamed of your dirtiness no more!

BENNY (*in a snarling whisper*). That's right! Blame it all on me. I s'pose she ain't got nothin' to do with it. (*With a wink.*) You oughter see her perform sometimes. You'd get wise to something then.

HARRIET. Shut up! You've the same filthy mind your Pa had. As for Emmer, I don't hold her responsible. She's been gettin' flighty the past two years. She couldn't help it, livin' alone the way she does, shut up in this house all her life. You ought to be 'shamed to take advantage of her condition—but shame ain't in you.

BENNY. Aw, give us a rest!

254

HARRIET (*angrily*). Your Uncle Caleb'll give you a rest when he sees you! Him and me's agreed not to give you another single penny if you was to get down on your knees for it. So there! You can git along on your army pay from this onward.

BENNY (*worried by the finality in her tone—placatingly.*) Aw, say, Ma, what's worryin' you? What 'ave I done that's so bad? Gosh, you oughta know some of the gang I know in the army. You'd think I was a saint if you did. (*Trying a confidential tone.*) Honest, Ma, this here thing with Aunt Emmer ain't my fault. How can I help it if she goes cranky in her old age and gets sweet about me? (*With a sly grin—in a whisper.*) Gee, Ma, you oughter see her to-day. She's a scream, honest! She's upstairs now gettin' calmed down. She was gettin' crazy when you're callin' stopped her. Wait till she comes down and you git a look! She'll put your eye out —all dolled up like a kid of sixteen and enough paint on her face for a Buffalo Bill Indian——

HARRIET (*staring at him with stern condemnation*). You're a worthless loafer, Benny Rogers, same as your Pa was.

BENNY (*frustrated and furious*). Aw, g'wan with that bunkum! (*He turns away from her.*)

HARRIET. And I'm goin' to tell Emmer about you and try to put some sense back into her head.

BENNY. Go ahead. You'll get fat runnin' me down to her!

HARRIET And if my word don't have no influence,

255

I'll tell your Uncle Caleb everything, and get him to talk to her. She'll mind him.

BENNY (*defiantly*). You just try it, that's all!

HARRIET. I've been scared to do more'n hint about it to him. I'm hopin' any day Emmer'll come out of this foolishness, and he'll never know.

BENNY. Aw!

HARRIET. If shame was in you, you'd remember your Uncle Caleb's been in love with Emmer all his life and waited for her year after year hopin' in the end she'd change her mind and marry him. And she will, too, I believe, if she comes out of this fit into her sane mind—which she won't if you keep fussin' with her.

BENNY (*with revengeful triumph*). She'll never marry the old cuss—I'll fix that!

HARRIET. Now you're showin' yourself up for what you are! And I kin see it's come to the p'int where I got to tell your Uncle Caleb everythin' no matter how it breaks him up. I got to do it for Emmer's sake as well as his'n. We got to get her cured of your bad influence once and for all. It's the on'y hope for the two of 'em.

BENNY. You just try it!

HARRIET. And as for you, you get back to the army where you b'long! And don't never expect another cent from me or Caleb 'cause you won't get it! And don't never come to see us again till you've got rid of the meanness and filth that's the Rogers part of you and found the honesty and decency that's the Williams part—if you got any of me in you at all, which I begin to doubt. (*Goes to the door in rear.*)
256

And now I'm goin' back to Caleb—and you better not let him find you here when he comes less'n you want a good hidin' for once in your life. (*She goes out.*)

BENNY (*stammering between fear and rage—shouting after her*). G'wan! Tell him! What the hell do I care? I'll fix him! I'll spill the beans for both of you, if you try to fix me! (*He stands in the middle of the room hesitating whether to run away or stay, concentrating his thoughts on finding some way to make good his bluff. Suddenly his face lights up with a cruel grin and he mutters to himself with savage satisfaction.*) By God, that's it! I'll bet I kin work it, too! By God, that'll fix 'em! (*He chuckles and goes quickly to the door on right and calls up to the floor above.*) Emmer! Emmer!

EMMA (*her voice faintly heard answering*). Yes, Benny, I'm coming.

BENNY (*he calls quickly*). Come down! Come down quick! (*He comes back to the centre of the room where he stands waiting, planning his course of action.*)

EMMA (*appears in the doorway. Her face is profusely powdered—with nervous excitement*). Benny! What's the matter? You sounded so—why, where's your Ma?

BENNY. Gone. Gone back home.

EMMA (*offendedly*). Without waiting to see me? Why, I only sat down for a minute to give you a chance to talk to her. I was coming right down. Didn't she want to see me? Whatever's got into Harriet lately?

BENNY. She's mad as thunder at you 'cause I come over here so much 'stead of stayin' home with her.

257

EMMA (*pleased*). Oh, is that why? Well, if she ain't peculiar! (*She sits in a rocker by the table.*)

BENNY (*with a great pretence of grief, taking one of her hands in his*). Say, Emmer—what I called you down for was—— I want to say good-bye and thank you for all you've done——

EMMA (*frightenedly*). Good-bye? How can you say that! What——?

BENNY. Good-bye for good this time.

EMMA. For good?

BENNY. Yes. I've got to beat it. I ain't got no home here no more. Ma and Uncle Caleb, they've chucked me out.

EMMA. Good gracious, what're you saying?

BENNY. That's what Ma come over to tell me—that Uncle Caleb'd said I'd never get another cent from him, alive or after he's dead, and she told me to git back to the army and never to come home again.

EMMA (*gasping*). She was only joking. She—they couldn't mean it.

BENNY. If you'd heard her you wouldn't think she was joking.

EMMA (*as he makes a movement as if to go away*). Benny! You can't go! Go, and me never see you again, maybe! You can't! I won't have it!

BENNY. I got to, Emmer. What else is there for me to do when they've throwed me out? I don't give a damn about leaving them—but I hate to leave you and never see you again.

258

EMMA (*excitedly—grabbing his arm*). You can't! I won't let you go!

BENNY. I don't want to—but what can I do?

EMMA. You can stay here with me.

BENNY (*his eyes gleaming with satisfaction*). No, I couldn't. You know this sort of a town. Folks would be sayin' all sorts of bad things in no time. I don't care for myself. They're all down on me anyway because I'm diff'rent from small-town boobs like them and they hate me for it.

EMMA. Yes, you are diff'rent. And I'll show 'em I'm diff'rent, too. You can stay with me—and let 'em gossip all they've a mind to!

BENNY. No, it wouldn't be actin' square with you. I got to go. And I'll try to save up my pay and send you back what I've borrowed now and again.

EMMA (*more and more wrought up*). I won't hear of no such thing. Oh, I can't understand your Ma and your Uncle Caleb bein' so cruel!

BENNY. Folks have been lyin' to her about me, like I told you, and she's told him. He's only too glad to believe it, too, long as it's bad.

EMMA. I can talk to your Uncle Caleb. He's always minded me more'n her.

BENNY (*hastily*). Don't do that, for God's sake! You'd only make it worse and get yourself up against him, too!

EMMA (*bewilderedly*). But—I—don't see——

259

BENNY (*roughly*). Well, he's still stuck on you, ain't he?

EMMA. (*with a flash of coquetry*). Now, Benny!

BENNY. I ain't kiddin'. This is dead serious. He's stuck on you and you know it.

EMMA (*coyly*). I haven't given him the slightest reason to hope in thirty years.

BENNY. Well, he hopes just the same. Sure he does! Why, Ma said when she was here just now she'd bet you and him'd be married some day yet

EMMA. No such thing! Why, she must be crazy!

BENNY. Oh, she ain't so crazy Ain't he spent every durn evenin' of the time he's home between trips, over here with you—for the last thirty years?

EMMA. When I broke my engagement I said I wanted to stay friends like we'd been before, and we always have; but every time he'd even hint at bein' engaged again I'd always tell him we was friends only and he'd better leave it be that way. There's never been nothing else between us. (*With a coy smile.*) And besides, Benny, you know how little time he's had at home between viges.

BENNY. I kin remember the old cuss marchin' over here every evenin' he was home since I was a kid.

EMMA (*with a titter of delight*). D'you know, Benny, I do actually believe you're jealous!

BENNY (*loudly—to lend conviction*). Sure I'm jealous! But that ain't the point just now. The point is *he's* jealous of me—and you can see what chance you've
260

got of talkin' him over now, can't you! You'd on'y make him madder.

EMMA (*embarrassedly*). He's getting foolish. What cause has he got——

BENNY. When Ma tells him the lies about us——

EMMA (*excitedly*). What lies?

BENNY. I ain't goin' to repeat 'em to you, but you kin guess, can't you, me being so much over here?

EMMA (*springing to her feet—shocked but pleased*). Oh!

BENNY (*turning away from her*). And now I'm going to get out. I'll stay at Bill Grainger's to-night and get the morning train.

EMMA (*grabbing his arm*). No such thing! You'll stay right here!

BENNY. I can't—Emmer. If you was really my aunt, things'd be diff'rent and I'd tell 'em all to go to hell.

EMMA (*smiling at him coquettishly*). But I'm glad I ain't your aunt.

BENNY. Well, I mean if you was related to me in some way. (*At some noise he hears from without, he starts frightenedly.*) Gosh, that sounded like our front door slamming. It's him and he's coming over. I got to get out the back way. (*He starts for the door on the right.*)

EMMA (*clinging to him*). Benny! Don't go! You musn't go!

BENNY (*inspired by alarm and desire for revenge suddenly blurts out*). Say, let's me 'n' you git married, Emmer—to-morrow, eh? Then I kin stay! That'll stop 'em, damn 'em, and make 'em leave me alone.

261

EMMA (*dazed with joy*). Married ? You 'n' me ? Oh, Benny, I'm too old. (*She hides her head on his shoulder.*)

BENNY (*hurriedly, with one anxious eye on the door*). No, you ain't ! Honest, you ain't ! You're the best girl in this town ! (*Shaking her in his anxiety.*) Say yes, Emmer ! Say you will—first thing to-morrow.

EMMA (*choking with emotion*). Yes—I will—if I'm not too old for you.

BENNY (*jubilantly*). Tell him. Then he'll see where he gets off ! Listen ! I'm goin' to the kitchen and wait. You come and tell me when he's gone. (*A knock comes at the door. He whispers.*) That's him. I'm goin'.

EMMA (*embracing him fiercely*). Oh, Benny ! (*She kisses him on the lips. He ducks away from her and disappears off right. The knock is repeated. Emma dabs tremblingly at her cheeks with a handkerchief. Her face is beaming with happiness and looks indescribably silly. She trips lightly to the door and opens it— forcing a light, careless tone.*) Oh, it's you, Caleb. Come right in and set. I was kind of expecting you. Benny—I'd heard that you was due home to-night.

> (*He comes in and shakes the hand she holds out to him in a limp, vague, absent-minded manner. In appearance, he has changed but little in the thirty years save that his hair is now nearly white and his face more deeply lined and wrinkled. His body is still erect, strong and vigorous. He wears dark clothes, much the same as he was dressed in Act One.*)

CALEB (*mechanically*). Hello, Emmer.

> (*Once inside the door, he stands staring about
> the room, frowning. The garish strange-
> ness of everything evidently repels and
> puzzles him. His face wears its set
> expression of an emotionless mask, but his
> eyes cannot conceal an inward struggle,
> a baffled and painful attempt to com-
> prehend, a wounded look of bewildered hurt.*)

EMMA (*blithely indifferent to this—pleasantly*). Are
you looking at the changes I've made ? You ain't
seen this room since, have you ? Of course not.
What am I thinking of ? They only got through
with the work two weeks ago. Well, what d' you
think of it ?

CALEB (*frowning—hesitatingly*). Why—it's—all
right, I reckon.

EMMA. It was so gloomy and old-timey before, I
just couldn't bear it. Now it's light and airy and
young-looking, don't you think ? (*With a sigh.*) I
suppose Pa and Ma turned over in their graves.

CALEB (*grimly*). I reckon they did, too.

EMMA. Why, you don't mean to tell me you don't
like it neither, Caleb ? (*Then as he doesn't reply—
resentfully.*) Well, you always was a silly, old-fashioned
critter, Caleb Williams, same as they was. (*She plumps
herself into a rocker by the table—then, noticing the lost
way in which he is looking about him.*) Gracious,
why don't you set, Caleb ? You give me the fidgets
standing that way ! You ain't a stranger that's got
to be invited, are you ? (*Then suddenly realising the*

263

*cause of his discomfiture, she smiles pityingly, not with-
out a trace of malice.)* Are you looking for your old chair
you used to set in ? Is that it ? Well, I had it put
up in the attic. It didn't fit in with them new things.

CALEB *(dully).* No, I s'pose it wouldn't.

EMMA *(indicating a chair next to hers).* Do set
down and make yourself at home. *(He does so gingerly.
After a pause she asks perfunctorily.)* Did you have
good luck this voyage ?

CALEB *(again dully).* Oh, purty fair.

> *(He begins to look at her as if he were seeing
> her for the first time, noting every detail
> with a numb, stunned astonishment.)*

EMMA. You're looking as well as ever.

CALEB *(dully).* Oh, I ain't got nothin' to complain of.

EMMA. You're the same as me, I reckon. *(Happily.)*
Why, I seem to get feelin' younger and more lively
every day, I declare I do. *(She becomes uncomfortably
aware of his examination—nervously.)* Gracious,
what you starin' at so ?

CALEB *(brusquely blurting out his disapproval).* You've
changed, Emmer—changed so I wouldn't know you,
hardly.

EMMA *(resentfully).* Well, I hope you think it's for
the best.

CALEB *(evasively).* I ain't enough used to it yet—
to tell.

EMMA *(offended).* I ain't old-timey and old-maidy
like I was, I guess that's what you mean. Well, I
just got tired of mopin' alone in this house, waiting
for death to take me and not enjoyin' anything. I
264

was gettin' old before my time. And all at once I saw what was happenin' and I made up my mind I was going to get some fun out of what Pa'd left me while I was still in the prime of life, as you might say.

CALEB (*severely*). Be that paint and powder you got on your face, Emmer?

EMMA (*embarrassed by this direct question*). Why, yes—I got a little mite—it's awful good for your complexion, they say—and in the cities now all the women wears it.

CALEB (*sternly*). The kind of women I've seed in cities wearin' it—— (*He checks himself and asks abruptly*). Warn't your hair turnin' grey last time I was home?

EMMA (*flustered*). Yes—yes—so it was—but then it started to come in again black as black all of a sudden.

CALEB (*glancing at her shoes, stockings and dress*). You're got up in them things like a young girl goin' to a dance.

EMMA (*forcing a defiant laugh*). Maybe I will go soon's I learn—and Benny's goin' to teach me.

CALEB (*keeping his rage in control—heavily*). Benny——

EMMA (*suddenly bursting into hysterical tears*). And I think it's real mean of you, Caleb—nasty mean to come here on your first night home—and—make—fun—of—my—clothes—and everything. (*She hides her face in her hands and sobs.*)

CALEB (*overcome by remorse—forgetting his rage instantly—gets up and pats her on the shoulder—with rough tenderness*). Thar, thar, Emmer! Don't cry,

265

now! I didn't mean nothin'. Don't pay no 'tention to what I said. I'm a durned old fool! What the hell do I know o' women's fixin's anyhow? And I reckon I be old-fashioned and set in my ideas.

EMMA (*reassured—pressing one of his hands gratefully*). It hurts—hearing you say—me 'n' you such old friends and——

CALEB. Forgit it, Emmer. I won't say no more about it. (*She dries her eyes and regains her composure. He goes back to his seat, his face greatly softened, looking at her with the blind eyes of love. There is a pause. Finally, he ventures in a gentle tone*). D'you know what time this be, Emmer?

EMMA (*puzzled*). I don't know exactly, but there's a clock in the next room.

CALEB (*quickly*). Hell, I don't mean that kind o' time. I mean—it was thirty years ago this spring.

EMMA (*hastily*). Gracious, don't let's talk of that. It only gets me thinking how old I am.

CALEB (*with an affectionate smile*). We both got to realise now and then that we're gettin' old.

EMMA (*bridling*). That's all right for you to say. You're twelve years older 'n me, don't forget, Caleb.

CALEB (*smiling*). Waal, even that don't make you out no spring chicken, Emmer.

EMMA (*stiffly*). A body's as old as they feels—and I feel right young.

CALEB. Waal, so do I as far as health goes. I'm as able and sound as ever. (*After a pause.*) But, what I meant was, d'you remember what happened thirty years back.

266

EMMA. I suppose I do.

CALEB. D'you remember what I said that day?

EMMA (*primly*). You said a lot that it's better to forget, if you ask me.

CALEB. I don't mean—that part of it. I mean when I was sayin' good-bye, I said—— (*He gasps— then blurts it out.*) I said I'd wait thirty years—if need be. (*After a pause.*) I know you told me time and again not to go back to that. On'y—I was thinkin' all this last vige—that maybe—now when the thirty years are past—I was thinkin' that maybe—— (*He looks at her humbly, imploring some encouragement. She stares straight before her, her mouth set thinly. He sighs forlornly and blunders on.*) Thirty years— that's a hell of a long time to wait, Emmer—makin' vige after vige always alone—and feelin' even more alone in between times when I was home, livin' right next door to you and callin' on you every evenin'. (*A pause.*) I've made money enough, I know—but what the hell good's that to me—long as you're out of it? (*A pause.*) Seems to me, Emmer, thirty o' the best years of a man's life ought to be proof enough to you to make you forget—that one slip o' mine.

EMMA (*rousing herself—forcing a careless tone*). Lord sakes, I forgot all about that long ago. And here you go remindin' me of it!

CALEB (*doggedly*). You ain't answered what I was drivin' at, Emmer. (*A pause; then, as if suddenly afraid of what her answer will be, he breaks out quickly.*) And I don't want you to answer right now, neither. I want you to take time to think it all over.

267

EMMA (*feebly evasive*). All right, Caleb, I'll think it over.

CALEB (*after a pause*). Somehow—seems to me's if—you might really *need* me now. You never did before.

EMMA (*suspiciously*). Why should I need you now any more'n any other time.

CALEB (*embarrassedly*). Oh, I just feel that way.

EMMA. It ain't count o' nothin' Harriet's been tellin' you, is it? (*Stiffly.*) Her 'n' me ain't such good friends no more, if you must know.

CALEB (*frowning*). Her 'n' me nearly had a fight right before I came over here. (*Emma starts.*) Harriet lets her tongue run away with her and says dumb fool things she don't really mean. I didn't pay much 'tention to what she was sayin'—but it riled me jest the same. She won't repeat such foolishness after the piece o' my mind I gave her.

EMMA. What did she say?

CALEB. Oh, nothin' worth tellin'. (*A pause.*) But neither you nor me ought to get mad at Harriet serious. We'd ought, by all rights, to make allowances for her. You know's well as me what a hard time she's had. Bein' married to Alf Rogers for five years'd p'izin any woman's life.

EMMA. No, he wasn't much good, there's no denyin'.

CALEB. And now there's Benny drivin' her crazy.

EMMA (*instantly defensive*). Benny's all right!

CALEB (*staring at her sharply—after a pause*). No, that's jest it. He ain't all right, Emmer.

268

EMMA. He is, too! He's as good as gold!

CALEB (*frowning—with a trace of resentment*). You kin say so, Emmer, but the facts won't bear you out.

EMMA (*excitedly*). What facts, Caleb Williams? If you mean the nasty lies the folks in this town are mean enough to gossip about him, I don't believe any of 'em. I ain't such a fool.

CALEB (*bitterly*). Then you've changed, Emmer. You didn't stop about believin' the fool stories they gossiped about me that time.

EMMA. You owned up yourself that was true!

CALEB. And Benny'd own up if he was half the man I was! (*Angrily.*) But he ain't a man no ways. He's a mean skunk from top to bottom!

EMMA (*springing to her feet*). Oh!

CALEB (*vehemently*). I ain't judged him by what folks have told me. But I've watched him grow up from a boy and every time I've come home I've seed he was gittin' more 'n' more like his Pa—and you know what a low dog Alf Rogers turned out to be and what a hell he made for Harriet. Waal, I'm sayin' this boy Benny is just Alf all over again—on'y worse!

EMMA. Oh!

CALEB. There ain't no Williams' blood left in Benny. He's a mongrel Rogers! (*Trying to calm himself a little and be convincing.*) Listen, Emmer, You don't suppose I'd be sayin' it, do you, if it wasn't so? Ain't he Harriet's boy? Ain't I brought him up in my own house since he was knee-high? Don't you know I

269

got some feelin's 'bout it and I wouldn't hold nothing agen him less'n I knowed it was true?

EMMA (*harshly*). Yes, you would! You're only too anxious to believe all the bad you can about him. You've always hated him, he says—and I can see it's so.

CALEB (*roughly*). You know damned well it ain't, you mean! Ain't I talked him over with you and asked your advice about him whenever I come home? Ain't I always aimed to do all I could to help him git on right? You know damned well I never hated him! It's him that's always hated me! (*Vengefully.*) But I'm beginning to hate him now—and I've good cause for it!

EMMA (*frightened*). What cause?

CALEB (*ignoring her question*). I seed what he was comin' to years back. Then I thought when the war come, and he was drafted into it, that the army and strict discipline 'd maybe make a man o' him. But it ain't! It's made him worse! It's killed whatever mite of decency was left in him. And I reckon now that if you put a coward in one of them there uniforms, he thinks it gives him the privilege to be a bully! Put a sneak in one and it gives him the courage to be a thief! That's why when the war was over Benny enlisted again 'stead o' goin' whalin' with me. He thinks he's found a good shield to cover up his natural-born laziness—and crookedness!

EMMA (*outraged*). You can talk that way about him that went way over to France to shed his blood for you and me!

CALEB. I don't need no one to do my fightin' for

270

me—against German or devil. And you know durned well he was only in the Quartermaster's Department unloadin' and truckin' groceries, as safe from a gun as you and me be this minute. (*With heavy scorn.*) If he shed any blood, he must have got a nose bleed.

EMMA. Oh, you do hate him, I can see it! And you're just as mean as mean, Caleb Williams! All you've said is a wicked lie and you've got no cause——

CALEB. I ain't, eh? I got damned good cause, I tell ye! I ain't minded his meanness to me. I ain't even give as much heed to his meanness to Harriet as I'd ought to have, maybe. But when he starts in his sneakin' thievery with you, Emmer, I put my foot down on him for good and all!

EMMA. What sneakin' thievery with me? How dare you say such things?

CALEB. I got proof it's true. Why, he's even bragged all over town about bein' able to borrow all the money from you he'd a mind to—boastin' of what an old fool he was makin' of you, with you fixin' up your house all new to git him to comin' over.

EMMA (*scarlet—blazing*). It's a lie! He never said it! You're makin' it all up—'cause you're— 'cause you're——

CALEB. 'Cause I'm what, Emmer?

EMMA (*flinging it at him like a savage taunt*). 'Cause you're jealous of him, that's what! Any fool can see that!

CALEB (*getting to his feet and facing her—slowly*).

Jealous? Of Benny? How—I don't see your meanin' rightly.

EMMA (*with triumphant malice*). Yes, you do! Don't pretend you don't! You're jealous 'cause you know I care a lot about him.

CALEB (*slowly*). Why would I be jealous 'count o' that? What kind o' man d'you take me for? Don't I know you must care for him when you've been a'most as much a mother to him for years as Harriet was?

EMMA (*wounded to the quick—furiously*). No such thing! You're a mean liar! I ain't never played a mother to him. He's never looked at me that way— never! And I don't care for him that way at all. Just because I'm a mite older 'n him—can't them things happen just as well as any other—what d'you suppose—can't I care for him same as any woman cares for a man? And I do! I care more'n I ever did for you! And that's why you're lying about him! You're jealous of that!

CALEB (*staring at her with stunned eyes—in a hoarse whisper*). Emmer! Ye don't know what you're sayin', do ye?

EMMA. I do, too!

CALEB. Harriet said you'd been actin' out o' your right senses.

EMMA. Harriet's mad because she knows Benny loves me better'n her. And he does love me! He don't mind my bein' older. He's said so! And I love him, too!

CALEB (*stepping back from her in horror.*) Emmer!

EMMA. And he's asked me to marry him to-morrow. And I'm going to! Then you can all lie all you've a mind to!

CALEB. You're—going to—marry Benny?

EMMA. First thing to-morrow. And since you've throwed him out of his house in your mad jealousness, I've told him he can stay here with me to-night. And he's going to!

CALEB (*his fists clenching—tensely*). Where—where is the skunk now?

EMMA (*hastily*). Oh, he ain't here. He's gone up street.

CALEB (*starting for the door in rear*). I'm goin' to find the skunk.

EMMA (*seizing his arms—frightened*). What're you going to do?

CALEB (*between his clenched teeth*). I don't know, Emmer—I don't know—— On'y he ain't goin' to marry you, by God!

EMMA. Caleb! (*She tries to throw her arms about him to stop his going. He pushes her firmly but gently aside. She shrieks.*) Caleb! (*She flings herself on her knees and wraps her arms around his legs in supplicating terror.*) Caleb! You ain't going to kill him, Caleb? You ain't going to hurt him, be you? Say you ain't! Tell me you won't hurt him! (*As she thinks she sees a relenting softness come into his face as he looks down at her.*) Oh, Caleb, you used to say you loved me! Don't hurt him then, Caleb—for my sake! I love him, Caleb! Don't hurt him—

273

just because you think I'm an old woman ain't no reason—and I won't marry you, Caleb. I won't—not even if you have waited thirty years. I don't love you. I love him! And I'm going to marry him—to-morrow. So you won't hurt him, will you, Caleb—not when I ask you on my knees!

CALEB (*breaking away from her with a shudder of disgust.*) No, I won't touch him. If I was wantin' to git even with ye, I wouldn't dirty my hands on him. I'd let you marry the skunk and set and watch what happened—or else I'd offer him money not to marry ye—more money than the little mite you kin bring him—and let ye see how quick he'd turn his back on ye!

EMMA (*getting to her feet—frenziedly*). It's a lie! He never would!

CALEB (*unheeding—with a sudden ominous calm*). But I ain't goin' to do neither. You ain't worth it—and he ain't—and no one ain't, nor nothin'. Folks be all crazy and rotten to the core and I'm done with the whole kit and caboodle of 'em. I kin only see one course out for me and I'm goin' to take it. "A dead whale or a stove boat?" we says in whalin' —and my boat is stove! (*He strides away from her, stops, and turns back—savagely.*) Thirty o' the best years of my life flung for a yeller dog like him to feed on. God! You used to say you was diff'rent from the rest o' folks. By God, if you are, it's just you're a mite madder'n they be! By God, that's all! (*He goes, letting the door slam to behind him.*)

EMMA (*in a pitiful whimper*). Caleb!

(*She sinks into a chair by the table sobbing*

*hysterically. Benny sneaks through the
door on right, hesitates for a while, afraid
that his uncle may be coming back.)*

BENNY (*finally, in a shrill whisper*). Aunt Emmer!

EMMA (*raising her face to look at him for a second*).
Oh, Benny! (*She falls to weeping again.*)

BENNY. Say, you don't think he's liable to come
back, do you?

EMMA. No—he'll—never—come back here—no
more. (*Sobs bitterly.*)

BENNY (*his courage returning, comes forward into
the room*). Say, he's 'way up in the air, ain't he?
(*With a grin.*) Say, that was some ballin' out he
give you!

EMMA. You—heard what he said?

BENNY. Sure thing. When you got to shoutin'
I sneaked out o' the kitchen into there to hear what
was goin' on. (*With a complacent grin.*) Say, you
certainly stood up for me all right. You're a good
old scout at that, d'you know it?

EMMA (*raising her absurd, besmeared face to his, as
if expecting him to kiss her*). Oh, Benny, I'm giving
up everything I've held dear all my life for your sake.

BENNY (*turning away from her with a look of aversion.*)
Well, what about it? Ain't I worth it? Ain't I
worth a million played-out old cranks like him?
(*She stares at him bewilderedly. He takes a handful of
almonds from his pocket and begins cracking and eating
them, throwing the shells on the floor with an impudent
carelessness.*) Hope you don't mind my havin' a
feed? I found them in the kitchen and helped myself.

EMMA (*pitifully*). You're welcome to anything that's here, Benny.

BENNY (*insolently*). Sure, I know you're a good scout. Don't rub it in. (*After a pause—boastfully.*) Where did you get that stuff about askin' him not to hurt me? He'd have a swell chance! There's a lot of hard guys in the army have tried to get funny with me till I put one over on 'em. I'd like to see him start something! I could lick him with my hands handcuffed.

EMMA (*revolted*). Oh!

BENNY (*resentfully*). Think I'm bluffin'? I'll show you some time. (*He swaggers about the room—finally stopping beside her. With a cunning leer.*) Say, I been thinkin' it over and I guess I'll call his bluff.

EMMA (*confusedly*). What—do you mean?

BENNY. I mean what he said just before he beat it—that he could get me not to marry you if he offered me more coin than you got. (*Very interestedly.*) Say, d'you s'pose the old miser really was serious about that?

EMMA (*dazedly—as if she could not realise the significance of his words.*) I—I—don't know, Benny.

BENNY (*swaggering about again*). If I was on'y sure he wasn't stallin'! If I could get the old cuss to shell out that way! (*With a tickled chuckle.*) Gosh, that'd be the real stunt aw right, aw right. Oui, oui! Maybe he wasn't kiddin' at that, the old simp! It's worth takin' a stab at, damned if it ain't. I ain't got nothin' to lose.

276

EMMA (*frightenedly*). What—what're you talkin' about, Benny ?

BENNY. Say, I think I'll go over and talk to Ma after a while. You can go over first to make sure he ain't there. I'll get her to put it up to him straight. If he's willin' to dig into his pocket for some real coin —real dough, this time !—I'll agree to beat it and not spill the beans for him with you. (*Threateningly*). And if he's too tight, I'll go right through with what I said I would, if only to spite him ! That's me !

EMMA. You mean—if he's willing to bribe you with money, you won't marry me to-morrow ?

BENNY. Sure ! If he'll put up enough money. I won't stand him otherwise.

EMMA (*whimpering*). Oh, Benny, you're only jokin', ain't you ? You can't—you can't mean it !

BENNY (*with careless effrontery*). Why can't I ? Sure I mean it !

EMMA (*hiding her face in her hands—with a tortured moan*). Oh, Benny !

BENNY (*disgustedly*). Aw, don't go ballin' ! (*After a pause—a bit embarrassedly.*) Aw, say, what d'you think, anyway ? What're you takin' it so damned serious for—me askin' you to marry me, I mean ? I was on'y sort of kiddin' anyway—just so you'd tell him and get him ragin'. (*As she looks up at him with agonised despair. With a trace of something like pity showing in his tone.*) Say, honest, Aunt Emmer, you didn't believe—you didn't think I was really struck on you, did you ? Ah, say, how could I ?

Have a heart! Why, you're as old as Ma is, ain't you, Aunt Emmer? (*He adds ruthlessly.*) And I'll say you look it, too!

EMMA (*cowering—as if he had struck her*). Oh! Oh!

BENNY (*a bit irritated*). What's the use of blubberin', for God's sake? Can't you take it like a sport? Hell, I ain't lookin' to marry no one, if I can help it. What do I want a wife for? There's too many others. (*After a pause—as she still sobs—calculatingly.*) Aw, come on, be a sport—and say, listen, if he ain't willin' to come across, I'll marry you all right, honest I will. (*More and more calculatingly.*) Sure! If they mean that stuff about kickin' me out of home—sure I'll stay here with you! I'll do anything you want. If you want me to marry you, all you've got to do is say so—any time! Only not to-morrow, we'd better wait and see——

EMMA (*hysterically*). Oh, go away! Go away!

BENNY (*looking down at her disgustedly*). Aw, come up for air, can't you? (*He slaps her on the back.*) Buck up! Be a pal! Tell me where your drink is. This thing's got me so balled up I don't know how I stand. (*With sudden fury.*) Damn his hide! I bet he'll go and leave all he's got to some lousy orphan asylum now.

EMMA. Oh, go away! Go away!

BENNY (*viciously*). So you're givin' me the gate, too, eh? I'd like to see you try it! You asked me to stay and I'll stick. It's all your fool fault that's

278

got me in wrong. And now you want to shake me! This is what I get for foolin' around with an old hen like you that oughta been planted in the cemetery long ago! Paintin' your old mush and dressin' like a kid! Christ A'mighty!

EMMA (*in a cry of despair*). Don't! Stop! Go away.

BENNY (*suddenly alert—sharply*). Sh! I hear someone coming. (*Shaking her.*) Stop—now, Emmer! Damn it, you gotta go to the door. Maybe it's him.

(*He scurries into the room on right. There is a faint knock at the door. Emma lifts her head. She looks horribly old and worn out. Her face is frozen into an expressionless mask, her eyes are red-rimmed, dull and lifeless. The knock is repeated more sharply. Emma rises like a weary automaton and goes to the door and opens it. Harriet is revealed standing outside.*)

HARRIET (*making no movement to come in—coldly*). I want to speak to Caleb.

EMMA (*dully*). He ain't here. He left a while back—said he was goin' up street—I think.

HARRIET (*worriedly*). Oh, dear! (*Then hostilely*). Do you know where Benny is?

EMMA (*dully*). Yes, he's here.

HARRIET (*contemptuously*). I might have guessed that! (*Icily formal.*) Would you mind tellin' him I want to see him?

EMMA (*turns and calls*). Benny! Here's your Ma!

279

BENNY (*comes from the next room*). Aw right. (*In a fierce whisper as he passes Emma.*) What d'you tell her I was here for, you old fool.

(*Emma gives no sign of having heard him, but comes back to her chair and sits down. Benny slouches to the door—sullenly*). What d'you want, Ma ?

HARRIET (*coldly*). I wanted your Uncle Caleb, not you, but you'll have to do, bein' the only man about.

BENNY (*suspiciously*). What is it ?

HARRIET (*a bit frightenedly*). I just heard a lot of queer noises down to the barn. Someone's in there, Benny, sure as I'm alive. They're stealin' the chickens, must be.

BENNY (*carelessly*). It's only the rats.

HARRIET (*angrily*). Don't play the idiot ! This was big thumpin' noise no rat'd make.

BENNY. What'd any guy go stealin' this early—(*As Harriet turns away angrily—placatingly.*) Aw right, I'm coming. I'll have a look if that'll satisfy you. Don't go gettin' sore at me again.

> (*While he is speaking he goes out and disappears after his mother. Emma sits straight and stiff in her chair for a while, staring before her with waxy eyes. Then she gets to her feet and goes from window to window taking down all the curtains with quick mechanical movements. She throws them on a pile in the middle of the floor. She lifts down the framed pictures from the walls and piles them on*

280

*the curtains. She takes the cushions and
throws them on; pushes the rugs to the
pile with her feet; sweeps everything off
the table on to the floor. She does all this
without a trace of change in her expression
—rapidly, but with no apparent effort.
There is the noise of running footsteps
from outside and Benny bursts into the
room panting for breath. He is terribly
excited and badly frightened.)*

BENNY (*stops short as he sees the pile on the floor*).
What the hell——

EMMA (*dully*). The tally man's coming for them
in the morning.

BENNY (*too excited to be surprised*). To hell with
that! Say, listen, Aunt Emmer, he's hung himself
—Uncle Caleb—in the barn—he's dead!

EMMA (*slowly letting the words fall—like a beginner
on the typewriter touching two new letters*). Caleb—
dead!

BENNY (*voluble now*). Dead as a door nail! Neck's
busted. I just cut him down and carried him
home. Say, you've got to come over and help look
after Ma. She's goin' on alarmin'. I can't do
nothin' with her.

EMMA (*as before*). Caleb hanged himself—in the
barn?

BENNY. Yes—and made a sure job of it. (*With
morbid interest in the details.*) Know how he did it?
You know our barn. The same as yourn a'most.
Well, he got a halter—same as you got on your cow

281

—and he made a noose of the rope for his neck and climbed up in the loft and hitched the leather end to a beam and then let himself drop. He must have kicked in that quick! (*He snaps his fingers—then urgently.*) Say, come on. Come on over 'n' help me with Ma, can't you? She's goin' wild. I can't do nothin'!

EMMA (*vaguely*). I'll be over—in a minute. (*Then with a sudden air of having decided something irrevocably.*) I got to go down to the barn.

BENNY. Barn? Say, are you crazy? He ain't there now. I told you I carried him home.

EMMA. I mean—my barn. I got to go down——

BENNY (*exasperated*). Oh, hell! You're as bad as Ma! Everyone's lost their heads but me. Well, I got to get someone else, that's all. (*He rushes out rear, slamming the door behind him.*)

EMMA (*after a tense pause—with a sudden outburst of wild grief*). Caleb! (*Then in a strange whisper.*) Wait, Caleb, I'm going down to the barn. (*She moves like a sleep-walker towards the door in the rear as*

THE CURTAIN FALLS)